The Performing Life

A Singer's Guide to Survival

Sharon Mabry

THE SCARECROW PRESS, INC.
Lanham • Toronto • Plymouth, UK
2012

Published by Scarecrow Press, Inc.
A wholly owned subsidiary of The Rowman & Littlefield Publishing Group, Inc.
4501 Forbes Boulevard, Suite 200, Lanham, Maryland 20706
www.rowman.com

10 Thornbury Road, Plymouth PL6 7PP, United Kingdom

British Library Cataloguing in Publication Information Available

Library of Congress Cataloging-in-Publication Data

Mabry, Sharon.
The performing life : a singer's guide to survival / Sharon Mabry.
p. cm.
Includes bibliographical references.
ISBN 978-0-8108-8408-3 (pbk. : alk. paper) — ISBN 978-0-8108-8409-0 (ebook) 1. Singing—
Vocational guidance. I. Title.
ML3795.M174 2012
782.0023—dc23
2012016418

Printed in the United States of America

Contents

Preface   v

Acknowledgments   ix

I: Preparing for Success   1

  1   Get a Good Start!   5
      Learn Early to Persevere
      Collect Mentors
      Expand Your Horizons
      Reminders!

  2   Who Are You?   19
      Find Your Niche
      Declutter and Move On
      Know Your Maintenance Level
      Reminders!

  3   Tap into a Rhythm   27
      Eliminate the Negative
      Develop a Routine
      Don't Spill the Beans
      Reminders!

  4   It's a Small World   39
      What Not to Perform
      What Not to Wear
      What Not to Say
      Reminders!

  5   Project Your Best Self   55
      Know Your Stuff
      Get Organized
      Speak Up
      Reminders!

  6   It Takes a Village   71
      Be Collaborative
      Develop a Support System
      Toast Your Hosts
      Reminders!

  7   Create the Life You Imagine   95

Plan for Success
Develop a Workable Lifestyle
Design a Balanced Life
Reminders!

II: Coping with Success   **115**

8   Malfunction Junction   117
   Learn to Read Maps
   Beware of Alleys
   Check Equipment Twice
   Ignore the Dissonance

9   I Can't Eat That!   125
   Ask the Waiter Twice
   Have a Progressive Dinner
   Where's the Beef?

10   Sleep Is Not a Perk   133
   What Time Is It?
   Call for Help

11   In Sickness or in Health   143
   Choose Pets Carefully
   Know Your Blood Type
   Don't Panic

12   Surprise!   155
   Friend a Piano Technician
   Record at Your Own Risk

Appendix: Fifty Practical Pointers for Performers   163
Suggested Reading   165
About the Author   167

Preface

Over a thirty-five-year performance career, I have sung dozens of recitals; inhabited several operatic roles; soloed with symphony orchestras, choruses, and chamber ensembles; performed on National Public Radio; recorded LPs and CDs; danced and sung in shows at the Opryland Theme Park; and even stood on a small box under a huge microphone to sing over the radio when I was six or seven years old. You could say that I've done a little bit of everything.

I have had incredible moments of exhilaration during performances, times when I felt that my feet were floating ten inches above the floor as I left the stage. There was nothing like those moments when the music had flow and I was able to tap into levels of expression never felt before, without any feeling of battering against a wall. But there were times when I struggled to get through them, especially when some illness or fatigue invaded my body and there was little I could do about it except visualize success and forge onward. Most people who know me personally or have heard me perform would never suspect the frequent difficulties I had to traverse to "sing effortlessly," as one reviewer put it. Often, there were organizational complications going on behind the scenes, schedule or travel glitches, and physical challenges to overcome to appear strong, healthy, and confident during performances. Looking back on some of those events, I wonder just how I was able to pull them off.

I suspect the same is true for many performing artists. No one goes through life without being held back by an occasional unexpected stumbling block. Though some performers face many more quagmires than others, this does not mean that one should go into the profession expecting or anticipating the worst to happen. That outlook on life would certainly be depressing, suppress creativity, and cause one to fear every move or decision that needs to be made. No one should live that way. It would be unproductive and unrealistic and would present problems for those who seem to have that psychological bent. Rather, it is essential that singers should expect good things to come, visualize the life they want to lead, and work to design a life plan that promotes flexibility and fortitude to combat any unforeseen problems on the way to a successful career in performance. In that way, they are able to deal, realistically, with both the extreme highs and the extreme lows that come with such an exhibitionist profession and find a happy medium for expectations to sustain a career over a long period.

Having been a voice teacher and mentor for numerous singers planning a performance career, I know that most tend to focus only on the glamorous side of the profession and rarely plan for complications until it is too late, when stress, performance pressures, and a debilitating lifestyle catch hold and wear them out. The sooner that a performer develops workable solutions to problems, puts a support system in place, creates an enjoyable lifestyle, and learns how to maintain a positive attitude and healthy use of the voice, the better. All of these strategies will help combat the inevitable mental, emotional, and physical stress that will invade the performer's life at some point due to commitment demands, family issues, and other obstacles that life brings.

Young performers just starting out tend to feel a lot of pressure to succeed. It's no wonder, since they have to work very hard to get prepared for a performing career and receive criticism from every direction while trying to get established. They have to learn to be flexible and deflect negativity to maintain a happy emotional equilibrium. Once a performance career is up and running, the pressure can be even greater for the successful artist who must live up to the expectations of fans, managers, and those who know her or him by reputation alone and expect a topflight performance at every turn. That can place a debilitating psychological drain on a singer at any station in his or her career. It can take away the joy of performing and the clarity of musical expression, and it puts too much emphasis on pleasing others.

When I decided to write this book, I contacted several professional singers, many of whom are also voice teachers, to ask what kind of book they would like to read and what would be of value to their students who are planning performance careers. All of them are familiar with my writing style from reading my "New Directions" articles in the National Association of Teachers of Singing's *Journal of Singing* over a twenty-five-year period and my academic book *Exploring Twentieth-Century Vocal Music: A Practical Guide to Innovations in Performance and Repertoire*. They encouraged me to write as if I were talking to them and their students on a personal level, talking from the heart and the mind. They wanted me to give advice about how to implement, enjoy, and survive a life in performance from my experience and fill a book with as much insightful knowledge, laced with humor, as possible. The following are some of the comments from those inspirational people, several of whom have read parts of the book and made suggestions as it was being written.

One said, "Please don't write a dry, academic book that will sit on my shelf. We already have some good ones that we use as reference. Instead, tell the stories of your performing life and how you got through the hard times."

Another remarked, "Young singers need to see what the performing life is really like, with all of its high and lows, not just the glamour. We want to laugh, cry, get derailed with you, and rejoice when you get back on track."

A close friend said, "Tell us what you value most about your years as a performer. Show us how your innate humor got you through the worst of times and how your training supported you when there was uncertainty and everything was going awry."

I have set out to accomplish the commands of those whom I consulted. This book is not meant to be a memoir. However, it does contain elements of a memoir in that it is part advice, part guide that relates actual events from my performing life as they apply to crucial issues involved in preparing for and coping with a successful career as a performer. I want the information in this book to show young artists that a life in the performing arts can still be fun, fabulous, and rewarding even when faced with seemingly insurmountable challenges. One of the things that I know for sure is that I would not have achieved my performance goals without excellent vocal and musical training, a balanced lifestyle, good organization, the help of a strong support group, the generosity of people I met along the way, and lots of luck.

This is not a vocal pedagogy book—though many of the issues discussed relate to the use of the voice and the things that affect it—nor one that tells you how to write a resume, what kind of headshots you need, how to write a cover letter, or whether you need an agent, though those are facts every performer should know. There are other good sources for that information and other subjects not covered in detail in this book. Several books that I particularly like—that have had a positive effect on both my performing and my teaching—are listed at the back of this volume in a section called "Suggested Reading," along with an introduction concerning the types of books included and how they can be useful.

Primarily, this is a book about survival—public spectacle survival, which requires day-to-day persistence in the face of personal and professional pressures, expectations, illness, demands from the fans, and other distractions that can change the course of a particular performance or, ultimately, a career. It is about how performers need to bolster their mental, physical, and emotional being, a necessity for the development of flow in the performance process and how that can translate into a positive reaction from the audience. Since I am a singer, my approach to this subject is focused on the vocal art. But the ideas expressed here should prove helpful to anyone whose performing life is in the public eye and especially to those who teach and mentor them.

The following chapters offer suggestions for the growth and enjoyment of a performing life while maneuvering through all kinds of pitfalls that can occur on a daily basis. I laughed a lot while writing about my adventures and misadventures over the years. So the advice given here, taken from experience, is both serious and humorous. Some points are quirky tips, while others are fundamental and critical to the issues being discussed. Many include personal recollections of times when things did not go exactly as planned, attitudes had to be readjusted, schedules needed revision, the voice and body had to perform through challenging circumstances, and the only thing that saved the day was a well-fed sense of humor.

The book is divided into two parts. Part I, "Preparing for Success," brings attention to factors that every performer needs to address when embarking on a career of exhibition. I believe that extensive and thoughtful preparation is a crucial element in developing all aspects of a successful performer's career. Building, surviving, and savoring a long career, which may include personal setbacks out of the performer's control, is difficult without such preparation.

For many years, I have kept a diary filled with stories of how I survived and coped with particular eccentricities, snafus, or tragedies in my performing life. In part II, "Coping with Success," I offer these reminiscences on various issues that I encountered to show that one can persevere through the most difficult of times and come out on the other side having developed a satisfying and successful career filled with a love for performing, a lot of friends while doing it, and plenty of laughter to last a lifetime.

In addition, there is an appendix that contains a list called "Fifty Practical Pointers for Performers," to use as a quick reference for lifestyle considerations and strategies that will help get your performance career on track and keep it there.

Acknowledgments

I was fortunate to have been in the presence of several outstanding teachers in my formative years. Three in particular influenced my singing and helped to develop my talent as a performing artist. They were outstanding role models in my musical development and gave me tools that have served me well as a performer and teacher of singers. Although none of them are still around to read this book, they must be acknowledged. Their influence, kindness, knowledge, and encouragement were significant factors in my musical development.

My first teacher, from age six to eighteen, Eleanor Hickey, gave me a valuable start by stressing sight-reading and technique in voice and piano. She displayed an infectious love for music and made sure that I had every opportunity possible to learn to perform in public with ease.

Elena Nikolaidi, my voice teacher at Florida State University, was also a wonderful role model. She was an internationally known performer with a charismatic stage presence and magnificent voice. She knew how to captivate an audience with a slight move of the hand, the caress of a tone, or a color change in the voice. I learned a great deal about projection of texts, interpretation of musical line, and how to hold an audience in your grasp just by watching her perform.

I can directly connect my early professional accomplishments, a development of self-confidence, and the acquisition of numerous useful teaching skills to my association with Louis Nicholas, my voice teacher/ mentor during my doctoral work at George Peabody College. He freed my voice of tension, honed my language skills, and encouraged me to go my own musical way. He possessed all the attributes of the finest of teachers. But most of all, he cared about his students long after they studied with him. He not only encouraged my efforts in the early days and saw where my creative abilities needed to be channeled but also remained a stalwart supporter of my efforts in performance and writing until his passing, often sending me cards or letters of congratulations for recent accomplishments.

As I think back over a long performing career, I have to thank all of those people who helped facilitate my career: the generous hosts who housed and fed me and picked me up at airports and drove me to rehearsals in cities far from my home, the venue managers who arranged concert details flawlessly, the fine conductors with whom I have worked, and the many composers who allowed me to record and premiere their works. All of them helped to make my performing career more exciting, diverse, and pleasurable.

I must also thank my medical doctors who helped me get through several bouts of illness during the past thirty-five years that could have easily derailed my career. They were most considerate, knowledgeable, and available when I needed them. I was fortunate to find them.

I have had the privilege of working with many fine musicians during a long career in vocal performance. I appreciate the generosity and high-level musicianship of all of those with whom I worked on recordings, concert tours, and operatic or orchestral performances. But there are two collaborators who must be thanked above all others. Without them, this book and its content would not exist. These two women are extremely talented pianists who played on all of my major venue performances and recordings since the late 1970s. They are not just wonderful musicians but great friends as well.

First, I am most grateful to Rosemary Platt, a world-class musician who gave me the opportunity to record some fabulous music by women composers on her already-established recording series. She also joined me for the premiere and recording of Elizabeth Vercoe's *Herstory III*, a monumental effort that received outstanding reviews. We enjoyed several years of grand music making until she decided to retire from teaching at Ohio State University and teach in China. Unfortunately, that is just too far to go for a rehearsal and my loss. I miss her dearly.

Second, I am forever indebted to Patsy Wade, an incredibly insightful pianist who can coax that instrument into doing just about anything she wants it to do. She can read my musical mind and has been a marvelous musical companion and friend for the past forty years. I have had fantastic times with her, traveling around, laughing and crying at our follies, and experiencing what the performing life has brought us together. I can't imagine having had such an enjoyable performing life without her. I thank her for giving so much time to our collaboration. It has meant a lot. She was a great inspiration during the writing of this book, since she was there from my doctoral days to the present and knows every blip, joy, success, and failure that occurred since our first meeting in 1973. So when I decided to write this book, I asked her to jot down everything that she could remember about our adventures. Her hilarious notes from performance trips, as well as those that I had compiled over the years, are the basis for many of the stories recounted in the book. In addition, she read every word of the book for accuracy and tone.

A special thanks to several singers and voice teachers who encouraged me to write this book and gave insight concerning the kind of content they felt would be most useful to young performers and those who teach them.

I am deeply grateful to several other people who contributed mightily to the writing of this book.

First, to my writer's group: Ellen Kanervo, Melanie Meadow, and Ellen Taylor—all wonderful writers themselves. None are musicians, but they cheerfully read through all of my advice to singers and made helpful comments concerning grammar, form, and content. I promise to write fiction the next time for their enjoyment at monthly meetings. What friends!

Second, to Edward E. Irwin, professor emeritus of languages and literature, colleague, and friend, who gave valuable advice regarding grammatical and syntactical issues during the editing of the book. I am most grateful.

Third, to Sally Ahner: singer, voice teacher, composer, Alexander technique specialist, colleague, and friend. She read the book for form and content and gave excellent advice concerning performance truths and relevance of material to be included. A wonderful colleague!

Finally, to my husband, George Mabry: conductor, composer, singer, and professor emeritus. He read every word of this book several times for form, content, and storyline. But on a larger scale, he continues to be my best friend, the world's greatest supporter, and the person who for more than forty years has been there for me in every triumph or trial. I am blessed!

I

Preparing for Success

A wide-eyed young singer sits transfixed, rarely blinking, in a large sold-out concert hall, listening intently to every vocal coloration and watching closely every gesture and facial expression of a famous singer, such as Thomas Hampson, Dawn Upshaw, Bernadette Peters, or Audra McDonald. She turns to her friend and says, "I'm going to be up there some day, you wait and see." Scenes like this happen every day in the world of public performance. The performance bug has invaded the young admirer's body and mind. She is starstruck and completely taken over by the idea of being onstage. It is doubtful that she is thinking about all of the hard work and years of preparation that were necessary to bring her idol to such a high level of proficiency and prominence in the field of performance.

Magical performers like those are incredibly inspiring to singers of all ages, especially young ones, and spur them on to dream big dreams. It's especially powerful watching veteran performers—those whose careers have lasted for a very long time—when they still sound great, seem to approach the work with enthusiasm, and go out to every performance with joy on their faces. People such as Tony Bennett, Placido Domingo, and Frederica von Stade come to mind when I think of singers who have enjoyed long careers and continue to inspire young artists through their recordings, performances, and master classes. That's the kind of performer that all young singers should strive to emulate, not the kind that makes a big splash, blows out the voice in a short time, and is gone with a "Whatever happened to . . . ?" kind of career before age thirty or, in some cases, much sooner. Unfortunately, that question is asked more often than not about singers who seem to start off well and simply disappear from the radar.

There are many reasons for a truncated career. It's always nice if you can blame a lack of fortune on someone else. And, indeed, there are times when a singer's path is blocked by some obstacle beyond his or her control. But, realistically, some careers end early due to a young artist's lack of preparation, inflexibility, combative personality, or true understanding of what a performance career really entails, rather than some real or perceived evil force that stops it in its tracks.

Yes, the idea of being a famous performer is an exciting, powerfully addictive thought. But one cannot achieve it by magic or osmosis. Aspiring performers can certainly learn a great deal by listening to the greats in any genre, knowing every piece they sing, and hanging out with others who are totally absorbed with the music. But at some point, real work has to be done. New performers have to get down to the nitty-gritty details of building technique, musical skills, and the understanding of musical style to stand out from the crowd and not simply become a copy of that famous singer they so admire. Additionally, if attention isn't given to the development of their real life, the one offstage, the performing life may go bottom-up due to stress and the lack of a good support system or a workable and enjoyable lifestyle.

Some of the reality television shows that feature performers give the impression that one can just step up onto the stage and suddenly become a star. Even stars, though powerful, do explode. Besides, being a star is not the same thing as having a fulfilling performance career. Much of what we see on those reality shows is not truly reality. There's a lot of hard work and preparation, as well as meeting of the right people and the development of supportive and lasting personal relationships, that must go on in the background to get a career on solid ground. Even then, a lot of pruning, feeding, cultivation, and pampering need to take place so that the performer can meet the demands of the profession head-on, not feel overwhelmed by the enormity of the career's demands, and stay focused for any length of time.

Preparation involves many things, not just practicing technique, though knowledge and ease of technique are essential for any art. There is much more to consider. It involves the honing of mental, technical, physical, and social skills to survive as a performing artist. Grooming the body and mind is vital to success in performance, and it affects the facility of technique. Without thorough preparation, performers are constantly afraid to be "found out," to be faking talent and not worthy of any recognition they might achieve. That underlying insecurity can eat away at their confidence, preventing any lasting joy and fulfillment from performance efforts.

Singers are delicate artists, subject to despair at a moment's notice. They seem to need constant reassurance and approval from some entity in their lives. It is no wonder that this psychological need for praise develops. Their instrument is a personal, emotional one that is capable of revealing through its tone, color, strength, and stamina just how the day is going; it gives away the slightest change in mood, whether the singer wants it to or not. Since that is the case, a singer must find ways to make every day go as splendidly as possible to coax the voice into expressing itself in the most beautiful and freest way imaginable.

This section of the book brings to light many of the issues that I have found to be important to the development of a confident, lasting, and successful and joy-filled career. During my years as a performer and teacher of performers, I have come to realize that singers who are constantly battered about by criticism, never receive positive feedback, are left to dangle without sufficient psychological support, and lack good organization and interpersonal skills have a much harder time succeeding in the world of performance, perhaps in life in general. So, attention must be paid to these issues to launch a performance career and have it sail above water for many years. With good preparation, attention to detail, acquisition of competent advice, and the support of knowledgeable and caring counselors and mentors, a young singer can reach his or her goals much more easily than one who has given no thought to anything except becoming a star.

ONE

Get a Good Start!

There is no one route to success in the world of performance. Professional singers come from all kinds of places, large and small, remote and cosmopolitan, places that have resident symphony orchestras and opera companies and places where the local church is the only outlet for a musical experience. Some singers have expert training in music almost from birth, while others have to wait many years before finding their way around a musical score. They go to music conservatories where they receive more than one degree in vocal performance. Or, they go to small schools where they major in business until one day the university choir director hears them humming in the hall and says, "You have a great voice. Come join the choir. We need basses." Or, a friend talks them into trying out for the leading role in a local musical theatre production where the director takes them aside and, with sincerity, remarks, "You have a special talent. Once people find out how good you are, you will be in demand. You should do this full-time."

Those kinds of experiences happen regularly on the way to a performance career. They are life changing and cause people to rethink everything they know about themselves and the traditions with which they grew up. But at some point in their maturation, those singers who are meant to be performers discover they have talent, a voice, promise, charisma, and a drive to put all of that in front of an audience for display.

There is no doubt that environment plays a major part in the development of talent. In an ideal world, the budding performer would have ample opportunities to hear great singers both live and on excellent recordings, begin music lessons at a very early age, have outstanding teachers who are knowledgeable and encouraging, and have a family support system that underpins her or his every move both financially and psychologically toward a professional career in music. If a child who

5

grows up in a locale where there is little or no exposure to the arts and no one in his or her family feels that the arts are important to life's scheme, then it may be more difficult for a singer to realize the spectrum of possibilities for one's innate artistic talent. In that case, the discovery and grooming of musical ability and the possibility of becoming a performer could take longer, be circuitous, and happen only by accident or never happen at all. The performer may never know that she or he has what it takes to be a performer and may never experience that magical feeling when talent is exhibited to its zenith before an appreciative audience.

A lack of exposure to the arts does not mean that a young singer—who had little early training, who did not grow up in a city that is an arts mecca, or who did not have parents who played several instruments and listened to classical recordings day and night—is less talented than the singer who has been deluged by opportunities and positive musical influences. But it probably means that her or his performance skills have not been honed and that she or he will have to work harder to catch up to those equally talented singers who have come from backgrounds filled with musical advantages.

Even though musical snobbery does exist in the real world—the idea that one can make good musical contributions only if one has a certain musical pedigree—it is not important unless the singer makes it an issue and feels less of a person due to one's meager musical and environmental beginnings. But it may mean that a singer will have less confidence of one's ability to be accepted and thrive in the profession.

Even though singers with excellent natural talent might see themselves when reading that description of an underprepared singer, it is important not to fall into despair, to know that there is still hope for a promising future in performance. I have taught numerous voice students who came from rural settings and had limited instruction prior to coming to the university. Some have expressed their feelings of inferiority as they compared their musical experiences to others with whom they had become acquainted. They felt that the development of a thriving career in performance was hopeless in the face of such a musical and experiential divide. It is a struggle to play catch-up and cram what needed to be years of study and experience into a short period. However, I am happy to report that many of them have become fine performers and now sing professionally or eventually received doctoral degrees in voice and now teach at major universities. All they needed was good training, appropriate opportunities to showcase their talent, and a lot of encouragement to bring that talent and personal confidence level to its peak. So, with hard work and the development of a good self-image, musical starvation in the early years can be overcome.

LEARN EARLY TO PERSEVERE

Sensitive musicians need many things to succeed. They tend to internalize everything and feel that all criticism reflects on some inherent deficit rather than something that can be improved on with practice. So, it is ideal when one finds a teacher who is artistically skilled, versatile in one's approach to teaching, and nurturing when required by the student's temperament. The sooner that teacher is identified, the better, so that no negative attitudes toward performance are ingrained at an early age. I was fortunate to find such a teacher who understood and exemplified those traits, when my parents moved from the country to the center of a very small town, into a house across the street from the person who would guide me until I moved away to college.

Singers discover that they have a good voice and musical ability in many ways: a teacher notices that a certain child has a clear, strong voice in the first grade and that she can sing on pitch when the others cannot, or a church choir director points out to a parent that their son is a leader in the choir, gives him a solo for the Sunday morning service, and suggests that he take voice lessons. According to my mother, my singing career began at age three when I spent several hours a day whirling circles through the living room of our house while screaming like a siren until my attention could be diverted to something less earsplitting. This early foray into contemporary music and performance art was followed at age five by afternoons spent hugging the family phonograph that was exactly my height, a floor model that played 78 rpms of crooners from the 1930s and 1940s. By six, I could sing all of the words to "Racing with the Moon," "I Cover the Waterfront," and "Blackberry Boogie." Never mind that my voice was not in the same octave as those on the recordings, since they were all baritones.

Apparently, these early performances were enough evidence of "talent" to warrant music lessons of some kind. Or perhaps it was a less expensive alternative to therapy sessions for my parents. At any rate, I remember looking up at my mother and holding onto her skirt in anticipation as she called Eleanor Hickey, the local music teacher, to see if she would take me for piano lessons. When a "yes" came from the other end of the phone, my path was set. I just didn't know it then.

I started taking piano lessons at the age of six. Somewhere around nine, Mrs. Hickey discovered that I had "a voice." So, it was decided that I also needed a voice lesson each week along with piano. My parents were told that my progress was remarkable; thus, I was deemed "talented." *Was that a blessing or perhaps a curse?* It did not mean that I was just studying music as a hobby. Rather, it meant that I needed to practice diligently to play and sing ever more difficult repertoire. My mother determined that it also meant that I could practice and not have to make my bed, clean my room, wash dishes, or learn to cook, since I was going to be a musician. These were skills that I later wished I had been exposed to. But that's another story.

Students of all ages and abilities came and went from the white clapboard house opposite mine. Lessons took place from sunup to sundown five days a week and sometimes on Saturday. After all of this study, there had to be a time for evaluation and exposure to the public so that parents could see where their money was going—thus, the biennial studio recitals that allowed every student to have a moment in the spotlight.

There are events in one's life that will never be forgotten. It isn't as if you get up every morning with the picture of that instant in your mind. But you know that the slightest detail of the day could take you back there, causing unexpected images of the incident to flash through the neurons.

I still remember the lovely white three-quarter-length eyelet dress my mother bought me to wear. It seemed perfect for Schubert's "Ave Maria." We had searched for just the right dress for the spring recital held each May in the big auditorium of the city grammar school. There were pianists, violinists, singers, clarinetists, accordion players, and even a harpist. Mrs. Hickey could teach just about any instrument that a local child was interested in learning to play. My yearly performances there had gone well and mostly without kinks until the seventh grade and Schubert's "Ave Maria." What happened was unusual for me or anyone I knew. Perhaps it was an omen. I don't know if the word *omen* meant anything to me at that age. If so, I might have had an inkling of my performing life to come.

I recall standing at the door to the stage in the crisp white dress with my freckled face and newly permed hair. Earlier on the program, I had played a piano piece—no glitches—as usual. Now it was time to sing Schubert. This may have been the first time I can recall feeling jittery about performing. But I knew my song well and walked onto the stage at the gentle beckoning of my teacher, who was seated at the piano ready to accompany me. I remember her smile. I smiled back at her and out toward the audience as it applauded my entrance from the wings.

The auditorium was packed with relatives and friends of the performers. I caught a glimpse of my parents sitting in the back on the aisle. My mother was always a nervous wreck when I performed, and sometimes she had to stand in the hall until I finished. But there she was, peering around the head of a tall man seated in front of her.

All seemed to be quite normal as the introduction to the well-known Schubert song wafted from the piano. I had learned many useful things about singing by this time, details about clarity of diction, proper breath control, accuracy of pitch, and dynamic contrast. All of that mattered little because as I took my breath to sing the first note, the audience did not hear a beautiful tone escape from my slightly open mouth. No, it was a gulping, loud hiccup that emerged, not unlike the squawk of a large goose being strangled.

My goodness, the acoustics in that auditorium were exceptional. The sound reverberated off of every curtainless window and wall, the high plaster ceiling, wooden chairs, and hardwood floors. One could not hope for a more agreeable place to sing. I tried to continue, but the hiccups came faster until I had to close my mouth and hold my breath to keep the hiccups from escaping. By this time, Mrs. Hickey had stopped playing and was sitting quietly facing me, hands folded on her lap. With her usual composure, she turned to the audience and said, "Oh my, we'll have to give Sharon time to get over her hiccups and try this again a bit later. Not to worry." She started some feeble applause as I left the stage, mortified.

I was shocked, of course, but seeing the surprised look on the faces in the audience was even more frightening. Back in the anteroom, other students waiting to go on stared at me as if I had developed some incurable deadly disease. I headed quickly to a corner where I held my breath, raised my arms, crossed my eyes and toes, bent over toward the floor, and tried all of the other remedies that I could remember for getting rid of hiccups. After what seemed like an hour, they were finally gone. I tried very hard not to cry because I knew that my voice would not work if tears appeared. There was no mirror backstage nor a water source, since these were the olden days before singers carried water bottles everywhere, as if they were an extra appendage.

My throat felt parched from all the breath holding when the door to the stage opened and Mrs. Hickey leaned in and motioned for me to follow her out. She took my hand as we walked to the middle of the stage, whispering in my ear, "Everything will be just fine. Are you ready?" I looked up at her confident smile and said "yes," and off we went to a hiccupless rendition of Schubert's classic, learning that with support and perseverance one can survive an unexpected disaster. In this case and many others during my formative years, I was fortunate to have an understanding, encouraging, and adept teacher who took every little mistake with a grain of salt, never scolded or belittled me, and immediately provided other opportunities for me to have positive performance outcomes so that I would not dwell on anything negative. Though, I must say, for several years after that and even on occasion throughout my life, my mind wondered if those hiccups were lurking somewhere, waiting for a chance to be onstage again.

COLLECT MENTORS

Every singer needs to search for the very best and most supportive mentors possible when considering long- or short-term study of any kind.

Sometimes that kind of teacher is hard to locate immediately. There may be no one in your town that fits those standards. But with some serious investigation, it is often possible to find a teacher in a nearby town who can take you to the next level of musical achievement. So be vigilant. Don't stop looking. Ask everyone you know who has any connection with music: local high school choral directors, church choir directors, friends who study piano or other instruments. It may require getting on a bus to travel there for lessons. I know singers who have done just that. But it was worth the effort. One should move on if he or she feels that time is being wasted with a particular teacher, when no progress is being made, or if every lesson ends in a depressed feeling about the future.

Pay attention to how your voice and musical skills are progressing. It is important to do a regular personal evaluation. Is your voice working easier, gaining strength and range, and acquiring more flexibility? Are you learning appropriate repertoire for your voice? Are your musical skills improving? Do you feel more confident about your performing ability? If the answer is no or if you are experiencing vocal decline or even painful vocalization—a red flag—then you have to find another teacher as soon as possible.

Another consideration that is important to the learning process is whether you are being subjected to mental abuse through the teaching techniques of the teacher with whom you study. Unfortunately, some teachers lack good teaching skills and resort to brute force, shouting, denigration, and even physical abuse. None of which are appropriate means by which to learn to sing with ease. The voice will react badly to any of those approaches. Constructive criticism is necessary in the learning process, and all students must strive to incorporate that kind of information into their daily practice sessions and properly channel it toward a better performance outcome. No one should be held captive by physical or mental abuse. Get away from that kind of person immediately. Find someone who will accentuate the positive and eliminate the negative from the learning process.

A teacher can be quite humane while bringing a student to the forefront of his or her art. Too many musicians have suffered from private instructors of the opposite type, who exact perfection without joy of any kind. As recent articles on the subject in major vocal publications have said, "Enough already! No one should allow himself to be abused for his art." Rather, every artist needs to be exposed to creative teachers who will take the time to find out about individual student needs and learning methods and teach from a point of positive reinforcement rather than negative derision. This approach is more likely to get the artist's mind off dead center and moving toward exciting, creative goals.

I recall a conversation with one of my former students who had received her undergraduate degree at my university. She was an excellent singer who had won several major competitions. She was intelligent and had a sweet personality, with much potential to be a performer. Upon graduation, she went for a graduate degree in vocal performance at a major university, having received a full scholarship. I assumed that she was doing well until I received a phone call from her late one night near the end of her first semester there. She was in tears and could hardly speak. After a few minutes, I understood the problem but could hardly believe my ears. Apparently, her voice teacher, someone who was well established at that university, had screamed at her several times, pushed her against the wall when she made a mistake, and actually threw a book at her, just barely missing her head. She could no longer sing as she had. Her voice had closed up from fear that every sound she made would bring on some assault from this out-of-control teacher. She asked my advice, and I suggested that she speak to the chair of the department or the dean as soon as possible to get out of that teacher's studio. Unfortunately, she got no help there and had to stay in that studio until the end of the year. By that time, this normally self-confident singer had become afraid of her shadow and wanted to stop singing altogether. It took two years, a change of schools, and another teacher before she regained her love of singing and the beautiful, expressive voice that I once knew. This kind of situation is not isolated. Mental or physical abuse should not be tolerated by a student or any institution that offers educational opportunities.

I grew up in Newport, a small town of approximately twelve thousand residents in East Tennessee. It is a beautiful place, right at the foot of the Smoky Mountains, with vistas that take your breath away. I know that much of who and what I am today belongs to that time, those growing-up years, and the people who helped shape my talent and mind. There is no reason to believe that in a little isolated rural community one would find spectacular educational experiences. But I did! I lived two blocks from the city elementary school, where I studied in self-contained classrooms, having only one teacher each year through the eighth grade. Two blocks in the other direction from my house was the high school, which took me through my last four years in Newport before I went away to college. I vividly remember individual teachers during those years, teachers who spent extra time with this shy only child who needed to learn how to play with others, speak confidently and distinctly in class, become an independent thinker, and stop worrying about almost everything.

I credit my sixth-grade teacher for giving me much of the information that one needs to get along in life, such as how to be a good citizen and stay out of jail and how to present oneself in public with authority and confidence. Yes, Miss Elizabeth Thomas taught every student in the class, boys and girls, how to write a check, make change correctly, answer the phone with a pleasant voice, answer the door safely while being wary of strangers, introduce people to each other with proper etiquette, set a fine dinner table as if planning a six-course meal—a table was always in the back of the classroom ready to be set for the day, and a different student was assigned to the task each morning—how to speak in front of the class with proper facial expressions, demeanor, and diction, though no attempt was made to rub out the rather thick East Tennessee accent. That was something I had to learn much later at a university in a different state. Finally, she spent a lot of time trying to teach us how to treat each other with respect. There were a lot of lessons dealing with "please" and "thank you." She expected the very best from each of us and made us feel that we were able to achieve it. Those lessons have served me well and have been referred to on many occasions in my performing career and personal life.

There were other special teachers along the way—the algebra teacher who tutored me at her home on Wednesday nights, gave me cookies and ice cream, and was oh-so-patient when I would say, "But I just don't see why x should equal whatever it is supposed to equal." She managed to drill enough math into my head to get me out of sophomore algebra with a C, the lowest grade I made in any class in high school. And her final career choice words to me were, "You've worked really hard on this and given your very best in this subject, but I advise you to stay away from math from now on if at all possible." She added, "You do sing, don't you?" Fortunately, for all other math teachers, I never had to take another math course and, yes, I do sing.

I was taught a good lesson in dramatics and physical balance from my senior history teacher. I was in class the day that she stood on top of her desk, acting out one of Napoleon's battles. Unfortunately, she took one step too far to the right and fell off and sprained her wrist. Never fear, she was back in class the next day, continuing the battle with even more gusto. Believe me, no one ever fell asleep in her class, and no one skipped it because you somehow knew that she would miss you if your seat was empty and no one wanted to disappoint Mrs. Babb.

Yes, my house was between those two schools. I could see both of them from my front porch. But directly across the street from my house was that other house, the one filled with music that poured out of the open windows and was heard all around the block. It was coming from the home of Eleanor Hickey.

Every artist needs a confidant, a mentor. Mrs. Hickey was that person in my life until I moved away to college. Her house became my sanctuary. She was my lifeline in so many ways: understanding that I needed early support to build confidence, encouraging me when I felt defeated by the slightest musical task, taking me to National Federation of Music Clubs competitions to try out my luck and hear musicians from a larger geographical area, teaching piano facility and music reading skills that would underpin a strong musicianship, providing opportunities to perform for local civic groups and other venues, introducing me to professional musical offerings not available in my city, giving advice about where I might go to college for further training, and feeding me home-made biscuits and fried rabbit for breakfast when my piano lesson was scheduled at 7:30 in the morning before going to school. I was blessed.

She taught me much more than piano and voice. She showed me the positive impact that a teacher can make on raw talent, on thinking patterns, on social development, and on the development of a career. She constantly spoke of excellence. We were never allowed to believe that we could be ordinary. I recall her voice saying, "If you *think* you will do well, then you *will*. If you *think* you will fail, then you *might*." She was kind, generous, and devoted to her students but exacted from them every ounce of talent that could be brought to the surface.

Though I completed an undergraduate degree at one of the major music schools in the United States and received excellent instruction, I graduated feeling directionless and goalless and had not greatly improved my performance skills in voice to the level necessary for a performance career. So, I concentrated on piano at the master's level and didn't study voice at all for a few years. I had lost my delight for performance and confidence as a singer.

I can directly connect my early professional accomplishments as a singer, an improvement in self-confidence, and the acquisition of numerous useful teaching skills to my association with the next and final teacher-mentor, Louis Nicholas, my voice teacher during my doctoral work at George Peabody College. I'll never forget the first time I sang for him. My accompanist, Patsy Wade, and I went to his office, a large, dark, paneled room in an old building at Peabody. There were numerous pictures of famous musicians on the walls, a grand piano draped with a large table rug, and several comfortable chairs. He was a small, delicate man with a gentle demeanor, a quick step, and a lilt in his voice. He opened the door and said, "Come in, Shay-ron," a pronunciation of my name that I had never heard. Patsy and I had prepared several pieces to perform so that he could get some idea of my singing. I was very nervous since I needed to make a good impression to get into his studio for voice lessons. It was rumored that he took only the best students. I knew that I was *not* secure in my vocal technique, having concentrated on piano and studied no voice since leaving undergraduate school. In addition, I still felt that I might have just an ordinary talent for classical singing, nothing special. He made me feel at ease right away by asking about my background, previous studies, former teachers, and how I felt about my accomplishments. I tried to give honest answers but did not really let him know my true feelings about a lack of vocal progress and self-confidence.

I sang four pieces for him in different languages and musical style periods, one aria, and three art songs. When I finished, there was a brief moment of absolute silence. I didn't move and he didn't speak. Then he said, "Shay-ron, do you always sing like that?" Well, now you can take that two ways. You can assume that he thought you were really bad, to which you could say, "Oh no, I have a sore throat today, and this is not really how I usually sound." Or, you can assume that he thought you were fantastic, to which you would say, "Why yes, I always sing that well."

I really didn't know what to do for a moment, but I decided to simply tell the truth and say, "Yes, you heard the best I can do at this time." I was waiting for him to show me the door, but instead he replied, "Well, we have a lot of work to do because your French and German are unrecognizable and you seem to have a number of vocal problems that need to be corrected, but I can tell that you are a marvelous musician, have a fine voice, and there's nothing wrong that can't be fixed." Those words changed my entire outlook. He made me *believe* that I could be what I dreamed to be. I never looked back except to wish that I had heard those words several years before.

What is it about these teachers that made them so effective and so memorable? There are several things they had in common. First and foremost, they were highly intelligent people who were inquisitive about their subjects and about life in general. They never stopped learning. They had a zeal for knowledge that was infectious. They gave the impression that everyone else in the world was searching for excellence, so there was no reason to settle for less.

Each had the attitude of expectation, rather than a dread of daily teaching tasks. Each was extremely well prepared to teach his or her subject, having expertise that was evident in class lectures and coaching sessions and private conversations. Finally, each one was a master at finding a particular variation in a student that could be strengthened by persuasion and then rejoicing with that student when major breakthroughs in skills or knowledge occurred. Each knew that an artful critique focuses on what a person has done and can do, and none ever read a mark of character into a job poorly done.

Individuals learn in disparate ways, finding their own paths to knowledge. A teacher can merely be a guide through a convoluted maze of information and learning styles. This is where the young artist and those around him or her must work to find a flexible instructor/mentor whose teaching style allows for the acquisition of high-level skills while gaining emotional strength and confidence to perform successfully in front of a critical audience. Connecting the aspiring artist to the appropriate teacher is the most important but often most difficult task.

As a teacher myself, I have observed students as they physically, mentally, and emotionally change due to the influence of particular teachers. I have watched faces light up, listened to voices grow stronger, and noticed changes in body language due to a shift in attitude after being in the presence of certain teachers. It is something that I have felt personally, and I know that without the people whom I have mentioned in my educational career, I would not have had the productive musical life I have enjoyed.

In summary, finding a highly skilled, encouraging, and inspirational mentor is the first and foremost task that must be accomplished on the way to a satisfying life in public performance. This process must be considered carefully and monitored continuously so that a performer is not exposed to, nor stays too long with, a teacher who is abusive or allows natural talent to stagnate. Word-of-mouth recommendations and public reputation are often better sources than print advertisement when searching for the appropriate teacher. The mentor's job is many faceted and monumental, and it requires a lot of patience. But it is also powerful, life changing, mind expanding, and overwhelmingly satisfying when the young artist becomes a uniquely talented person who performs with joy, security, and enthusiasm due in part to the care, guidance, and teaching of a worthy mentor.

EXPAND YOUR HORIZONS

Performers cannot succeed by living in a vacuum. They must see what else is out in the real world, what the competition looks like, and determine just how much work it will take to meet the demands of the profession. This knowledge is crucial when preparing for auditions, conversing with professionals during job interviews, and appearing confident in front of an expectant audience.

Though it is important to have a mentor who is always on one's side, it is also necessary to seek out the opinions of others in one's field through master classes, coaching sessions, apprenticeship opportunities, summer young artist programs, and other kinds of activities that put the artist in touch with new ideas. Not every experience of this type will be fruitful, satisfying, educational, or helpful. In fact, some may present information and ways of performing that simply do not work for the artist and should thus be discarded.

It was 1979 when I became a scholarship student at the Franz-Schubert-Institut in Baden-bei-Vien, Austria, a seven-week summer vocal training program in the German Lied; I was delighted to have been accepted. It was my first foray into specialized study of that type and my first trip to Europe alone. Very scary! But I boarded the plane in anticipation of a wonderful learning experience. Having just finished my doctorate in voice, I felt fairly well prepared for whatever might come my way.

At that time, the program consisted of seven weeks of intense study with only three days off, a difficult and exhausting schedule. There were classes in German diction, poetry sessions, and many master classes, with new coaches arriving every three days or so. You were not allowed to sing the same song twice. So, any free time was spent learning new songs for the next master class at which you were scheduled to sing. I learned fairly quickly that each coach wanted something slightly different than the one before: seven coaches, seven different approaches (sing it shorter, sing it longer, more diction, less diction, smile, don't smile, too much personality, show more personality, dress sophisticatedly, show more skin). Patience and discovering how to be a chameleon were probably the most important lessons learned here. As one of my student colleagues put it, "if they tell you to paint it green, just ask what shade and move on."

I coped well, met some interesting new friends, learned mounds of useful information, and thoroughly enjoyed myself until a famous German soprano named Irmgard Seefried arrived for a three-day stay. It had been rumored that she was "difficult." I wasn't quite sure what that meant, but stories of how she had "whittled down" students in other settings made everyone nervous prior to her first class with the group of ten or so singers and six pianists.

When she appeared before us on that first morning, as if a malevolent apparition, the classroom was deathly still as she walked slowly to the front of the room, leaned against the grand piano holding a cigarette case in one hand, and said something like, "I don't know what you've learned so far. It doesn't really matter. You will never be the same once I am finished with you. My goal is to break you down and make you into my image of what you should be." My natural inclination toward anxiety automatically kicked into high gear, and all I felt at that moment was absolute fear. I looked at the soprano next to me, who had turned a sickly shade of gray while trying to smile.

I have a lot of EQ. I didn't know what that was back then, but I know it now. I have excellent emotional intelligence. I can usually feel others' emotions before they say a word and read their thoughts through their body language and facial expressions. That can be very positive in developing good relationships, or it can predict disaster. Unfortunately in this case, it was the latter.

I wish I could say that things went smoothly, but by the time I stood in front of the class to sing, one soprano had left the room crying; a tenor had cracked on every high note he tried to hit; and another mezzo had managed to get through a complete song without choking—but barely.

I announced that I would sing Brahms's "Wir Wandelten," which was received with the following response: "Let's see how far you get with this one." My accompanist began the introduction, after which I sang exactly three words before Seefried rushed forward to within three inches of my face and clapped her hands loudly, yelling "no, No, NO." I don't actually remember much after that, except that the more I tried to sing, the more my throat closed and the tone became small, shrill, and stuck somewhere behind my tonsils. I had determined that I would not let this person intimidate me. After all, I had just finished my doctorate and been through the fire of writing a dissertation, and I had been performing professionally for a couple of years. But no matter how hard I tried, she succeeded in doing exactly the opposite of what I intended: she intimidated me. I never got to the end of that song. I was stopped after every other note for a grueling thirty minutes, with others in the class wincing and looking uncomfortable, knowing they might be next. Some left because they just couldn't stand to watch anymore.

At the end of the class, she seemed taller after having chewed up four singers. None had improved—again, it was the exact opposite. But we were told that this was necessary and that tomorrow we would get another dose of enlightenment, which would heal us in some way. I remember feeling so drained that I went back to my room in the Studentenheim, got into bed, and slept straight through the late afternoon and evening, missing my poetry class and not having dinner (I never miss meals unless I'm near death).

I never attended another one of her classes, and I concentrated on other studies. Some of the other singers chose not to sing for her at all, and some did not return for a second class. By the third day, only four students were left in the final class. I'm not sure exactly what that took for them to continue, but I knew instinctively that if I returned, I would lose self-confidence and be physically ill by the end.

It is necessary to learn to accept constructive criticism to improve your performance. There will likely be a lot of it during the years of preparation for a career and beyond. Indeed, performing artists often continue to seek out expert opinions about vocal technique, musical phrasing, languages, stage deportment, appropriate repertoire, and other factors throughout their career to stay fresh, energized, and up-to-date. However, each artist needs to know his or her limit of exposure to pressure, criticism, stress, and information overload when working with new teachers and coaches. If the teaching style is contrary to your personality type and learning style and becomes psychologically distressing, then it's time to jump ship. To do otherwise may cause or worsen vocal or emotional problems unnecessarily. So, *be aware* and *beware* of people who seek to strip you of confidence to make clones of themselves or someone pictured in their minds. Since no two performers are identical in every respect, this false view may not suit you, and it may serve to destroy what you have already built.

To develop a unique, secure career that separates you from all others in the crowd, you must feel expert enough to take chances, experiment with new ideas, and rely on inner creative surges of expression. Only then will you and your art have matured beyond the student level. Though it is important to seek knowledge and advice from coaches and professionals in the formative stages of a career, the various opinions must be deciphered, sorted, and culled—you must choose those ideas that seem to make you stronger: technically, musically, and emotionally.

Additionally, there is a danger in continuing to race around from expert to expert for too long a time, trying to be a chameleon and assume every new vision presented of your talent. This can cause one to feel like a student forever; it can cause uncertainty to take hold; and it can cause the real inner core of talent and individuality to be hidden from public view, never to be fully expressed. Some singers who continue on this uncertain path into their thirties become depressed and never find a sense of self, ultimately leaving the performing profession behind. At some point, all artists must settle on a clear picture of themselves that they wish to project, find one or two mentors to reinforce that image without fear of criticism, and go full steam ahead no matter what other people say. Often, the most memorable and creative performers are the ones who step outside the box and design their own worlds of artistic expression, leaving the naysayers with open mouths of surprise and a secret wish that they had been part of the performers' skyrocket to success.

* * *

REMINDERS!

- Seek out highly skilled, well-recommended, versatile teachers.
- Take advantage of master classes or other learning opportunities.
- Find good mentors and use them regularly for support.
- Remember the good performance outcomes and don't dwell on mistakes.
- Don't allow yourself to be verbally or physically abused by a teacher.
- Know when to stop trying to please numerous "experts," and project who you really are as a performer.
- Discard advice that does not suit you or that causes a decline in your technical ability or the joy in your performance.
- Don't be afraid to step outside the box and project your unique artistic expression.

TWO

Who Are You?

A career in vocal performance is built on many things, not just the fact that you are born with a beautiful voice. There are many singers out in the world who have gorgeous voices, but they do not make lasting careers in the performing arts. The opposite is also true: there are singers who have thriving careers, yet their voices seem not to have anything particularly special to offer, making one wonder why they have achieved success. Obviously, there is more to it than just having a great voice. Other elements come into play: musicianship, artistic expression, charisma, intelligence, perseverance, a good business sense, and getting a break by making the right contacts. All of these are important but may or may not play a part in the success of a singer. There are no guarantees that any one element or any combination of elements will bring success. But without at least some of them, it will definitely be more difficult to sustain a career.

There is yet another aspect to building a performance career that is often overlooked—that of deciding just who you are and what you want to express and project as a singer. It is difficult to make those decisions and accomplish goals if you have little knowledge of the possibilities. To make those decisions, self-analysis, professional investigation, and a sorting out of options must take place so that your performance outcomes will be unique, not a carbon copy of some other singer that you have admired.

It is difficult to explain what one does as a performer, especially the process, when those around you have never themselves experienced the highs and lows of being a performer. Performers who mature among others of like understanding or experience have the advantage of camaraderie from an early age, a beneficial situation when embarking upon a career in the profession. It can provide constructive psychological support to an insecure budding artist.

I can speak from personal experience that it is challenging to pursue a musical goal that cannot be understood, discussed, or enjoyed by those closest to you. As a child, I never thought that my life would be what it has become. I had no frame of reference, since no one in my family made a living in the field of music, no famous musicians performed in my town, and the only relative who took up any kind of instrument on a regular basis was a distant cousin who played mandolin on weekends in a bluegrass band.

Classical music was not heard in my house unless I was playing it. My parents probably felt off-kilter. They did not understand what I was doing, though they were extremely supportive in providing the education needed to achieve my goals. I suspect that they would have been more comfortable with the idea that I might become a country or pop artist, forms of musical expression they were used to hearing. Instead, I morphed into a vocalist who spent her career singing contemporary classical music, a genre that prompted my father to ask, after he heard me sing the premiere of a new work, "Do you ever sing anything with a melody?"

During family gatherings, it was impossible to talk about the music I was performing without getting blank stares and lots of questions that were difficult to answer. I felt like an alien dropped onto the earth from some passing UFO. But, as I matured, married a musician, developed relationships with artists in my field of interest, and gained confidence in achieving performance goals, I let go of the fear of family rejection due to my professional choice and accepted the fact that none of us can truly know the inner workings of another person's world, no matter the profession. Once this realization settled into my psyche, family dinners were a lot more relaxed. I no longer felt the need to explain my art, and I spent time exploring other avenues for discussion.

Therefore, it is quite possible to thrive and persist as a performer while living among those who have no understanding or appreciation of the artist's talent. In this case, however, good outside role models and mentors are crucial to the development of talent and the continued inspiration of the performer. If none are available, enthusiasm may wither, and the unsupported budding artist may never reach an otherwise achievable goal.

As a teacher of young singers, I commonly encounter students who struggle with the same kind of situation that I had in my formative years. They feel unsupported and misunderstood because they have no relatives with whom they can talk about their musical lives. Sometimes they speak of outright hostility from family members about their choice of profession and a withdrawal of financial and emotional support for their efforts. That is a very difficult situation with which to contend, and it causes some singers to abandon their dreams. It is hard to stay on a creative path against such negativity. Hearing of my early experiences seems to be of help to them. Several students have expressed relief and a renewal of determination at discovering that older, mature professional artists have thrived without their family's comprehension of their efforts.

In the absence of familial understanding, the teacher/mentor can be a psychological lifeline that connects the singer to like-minded performers, provides inspirational options in thinking, introduces other means of finding emotional and financial support, and helps the individual to realize that most artists tend to be hypersensitive to criticism and rejection. Most of all, performers need to hear that they are quite normal in their response to a lack of familial psychological support and that, although it is difficult in the beginning, they will eventually find other advocates, who will be bolsters as they pursue their goals, thus no longer requiring constant appreciation from relatives for their professional choice. With this kind of support, performers are more likely to develop confidence in their artistic ability as well as personal worth.

FIND YOUR NICHE

To feel intellectually and emotionally energized while building a successful career, it is crucial for performers to find the right niche within the profession they have chosen. Some gradually develop a proclivity for certain kinds of performance art over a period of years, going through cycles of experimentation with various modes of performance or genres of music before settling on the one that brings out the best of their talent. This necessary process can be both frustrating and illuminating, and it requires patience. Others seem to know instantaneously just what they are meant to do. Whichever the case, without a clear direction for one's artistic endeavors, fear, uncertainty, and inertia can take hold, stalling the performer on the way to a successful career.

In the formative years, singers need to learn the standard repertoire and spend considerable time becoming familiar with the work of great singers, past and present, within genres of interest. But at some point, all singers must each develop their own performance persona, one that sets them apart from the pack and makes listeners feel that they have a special gift for expression. To do that, singers must learn to visualize the kind of singer they wish to be while performing the kind of music they love—not what someone else wants them to sing. They should certainly seek advice from respected authorities in the field and from like-minded people who have empathy with the process. But in the end, singers have to decide just what kind of music makes them happy and how they want to spend the rest of their lives. Otherwise, the profession will bring only drudgery.

Once that visualization and realization is in place, singers must be brave and forge ahead, try out musical ideas for anyone who will listen, and learn to talk about their musical interests with intelligence. All of this sharpening of innate talent and artistic expression helps to create a more defined self-concept so that the performer can face the challenges of the profession with confidence. In other words, after the investigation period is over and you have decided exactly what you want to do with your musical talent, don't just sit around and wait to be discovered or allow other people to make all of the musical decisions for you. Be proactive, start preparing for the future, and make connections in your field—no matter how small or large—to get your career off and running.

Though I began studying music at an early age, it was several years before I knew exactly what I wanted to do with the rest of my musical life. Finally, around age twenty-six, I felt the chains of musical boredom fall from around my musical neck, and I felt free to do what I had innately wanted to do for years. That happened when I began doctoral work at George Peabody College and met my eventual mentor.

"You don't have the chest for that piece," said Louis Nicholas after I tried out one of the famous mezzo-soprano warhorse arias during a voice lesson early in my study with him. My accompanist and I broke out in laughter at his remark. He wasn't talking about my chest voice, a part of my range that was secure and well connected to the rest of my voice. Rather, he meant that my physical size—a petite and boyish five-foot-three (perfect for pants roles)—and vocal characteristics were all wrong for the piece I was singing. It was much too heavy and dramatic for my natural vocal weight. The idea that I might actually play that character in the opera was absurd. I needed a repertoire adjustment in the worst way, an adjustment that I had wanted to make many years before. All I needed was permission to do it.

My early piano and voice training had been quite traditional, focusing on the classics: lots of Bach, Beethoven, Haydn, Mozart, and Schubert for the piano. Voice lessons centered on early Italian songs, English folk music, an occasional American or British art song, musical theatre pieces, French mélodie of Fauré and Gounod, and German lieder from Brahms and Schubert with a few light arias thrown in—normal fare for students of classical singing.

Though I could handle the piano literature technically, I felt emotionally and intellectually out of sync with much of it until I played several more contemporary pieces of Bartok, Khachaturian, Ravel, and Albeniz. These composers had written for my particular sensibilities, and I knew it innately. I was a more contemporary kind of girl. I wondered what kind of music in this realm was out there for the voice.

During my undergraduate study, I would go to the music library and search for anything that looked remotely "modern," something that had unusual music notation. It was better still if the composer was not yet dead. My practice time was spent going through these unearthed gems and deciphering the odd-looking scores. Occasionally, I would bring one to my voice lesson, hoping to sing it for my teacher. She tolerated my eccentricity for a short while but soon asked me not to bring any more of it to lessons, saying, "Don't waste your time on this trivia. There is no music after Brahms."

So, I became a closet contemporary music singer, sleuthing through library shelves and listening to every recording I could find by Jan De Gaetani and others who specialized in contemporary music. Then Louis Nicholas opened the door with his remark about my choice of repertoire and gave me permission to say, "I've always wanted to sing contemporary music. Would it be alright if I bring some to lessons?" He said that he had not coached much of that kind of music but it would be fine for us to investigate the possibilities. I remember leaving his office that day with a smile and going immediately to the music library for ammunition to bring to the next lesson.

Over the next three years, I sang a wide range of music from various musical style periods and languages that suited my voice, but I concentrated on twentieth-century works with his blessing, writing about Schoenberg and Copland as dissertation topics. Hallelujah! I had found my niche.

DECLUTTER AND MOVE ON

Young performers need to collect experience. It is crucial to experiment with as many kinds of music as possible to come to a decision concerning what fits a particular talent. But once a performer is able to clean out everything that does not fit, the sooner a personal musical expression will emerge and become meaningful and satisfying to the artist. Not only can decluttering give the performer a clearer sense of the right musical direction, but it can also provide a better view of the performer's artistry for those who are observing from the outside, including potential audiences, managers, publicity representatives, hiring entities, and recording studios as well.

There is a great sense of relief when you settle into a niche with less vocal and mental stress, no longer trying to force your voice and musical sensibilities into an ill-fitting mold. Your musical life begins to coalesce. Mine certainly did. My voice and mind became freer, and I no longer struggled against a vast amount of vocal repertoire available. I began to whittle down the long list of songs and arias I had studied, and I took off everything that did not suit me. My teacher and various vocal coaches gave advice. But I discarded many pieces on my own because I felt no real musical connection to them. They bored me, created vocal tension when I sang them, or did not show my voice in a particularly interesting light. All of those excised pieces were not forgotten. They were useful to me later as a teacher of singers whose voices were different from mine. So, time spent learning them was most valuable.

With a new direction came new opportunities for performance. It is amazing how word spreads when you become known for doing a certain kind of thing extremely well, perhaps something that no one else in the vicinity is doing. After I began to program contemporary repertoire on university recitals, master classes, and other local venues, other musicians in the area began to notice. Suddenly, I was being asked by young composers to sing their works: a new music ensemble in Nashville needed a singer; they hadn't been able to find one who would or could sing contemporary music. I was invited to sing two difficult works at an international electronic music festival held at our university, and I sang several featured contemporary works at two national conventions of the National Association of Teachers of Singing in 1976 and 1983. A well-known German lieder coach with whom I had studied was present at the latter. He made a point to see me after the performance, took my hand, and said, "You have found your niche. Keep singing this kind of repertoire. It is quite special for you."

All of this happened in a relatively short period. So, I went from feeling at sea to being the captain of my ship and fully aware of the final destination. Thus, I began to specialize in this repertoire and spent the next forty years studying it, singing it, and writing about it. What a happy result for me!

KNOW YOUR MAINTENANCE LEVEL

Several years ago, one of my British composer friends amazed me when I picked her up at the Nashville airport following a transatlantic flight from London. She had come to the United States to hear me sing the premiere of one of her works and planned to stay three weeks. As she walked toward me with a tiny black bag, I said, "Oh, I hope your luggage made it across the pond with you." She looked surprised and said, "This *is* my luggage. It's all I brought." I was speechless. I consider that low maintenance.

On another occasion, I helped a soprano friend load five bags of various sizes onto a large dolly at the Nashville airport—all for her three-day stay in town to sing a concert. As we got into the car, she wondered if she had brought everything she needed. Definitely high maintenance.

My husband loves to say that I consider staying at a Hilton "roughing it." I am a bit picky. There will be no student hostels or camping trips in my future, and I'm not the kind of singer who wants to travel to London for a three-week stay and take only a small carry-on bag. I wish I were.

Life would be much simpler. But I don't need five bags for a three-day trip either. I'm somewhere in between.

Performers starting a career need to consider their personal comfort-zone requirements. There will be many times when comfort is crucial as travel schedules, strange accommodations, late or long rehearsals, teaching sessions, reception lines, public talks, interviews, parties, recording sessions, and other distractions infringe on the actual performance.

How needy are you? Be realistic! The amount of luggage you take on a trip is only one consideration when deciding if you are high or low maintenance. Do you require constant attention and support from friends, family, and hosts, or are you self-sufficient and need little to keep you on track? Knowing ahead of time what you require to have an enjoyable, stress-free performance will pay dividends when the concert actually takes place.

Singers have a multitude of performance fetishes that must be addressed to be psychologically ready to perform. Those who are completely tied up in elaborate preparatory rituals will have a harder time coping when situations don't go as planned. A good way to start thinking about this issue is to make a list of all of the things you require before a performance. They could include a specific diet, a smooth travel schedule, alone time, ideal sleeping schedule and accommodations, exercise time and space, optimum rehearsal and warm-up time, attention to chronic health issues, and the amount of time and energy you are willing to give to socializing with hosts and the public. Don't be fooled into thinking that you can easily change your stripes after years of the same routine. It probably won't happen, at least not overnight.

It is also helpful to make a list of situations and intrusions you wish to avoid before a performance. This list might contain items that affect the voice, your energy level, psyche, or general health: smoky or dusty rooms, cold air, talking too much or too loudly, certain foods, feather beds or other known allergy triggers, performance-day rehearsals, interviews, social events, and all scenarios that affect any personal eccentricities and performance rituals that are ingrained.

Study the lists carefully so that you get a realistic picture of who you are and what you currently think you need in order to go out into the world and appear to be professional yet relaxed in front of the audience. Notice how much baggage, both physical and psychological, you are carrying as the lists grow. Just be aware that the longer the list, the more psychological support you will need to reach artistic goals and get to the final destination intact.

As time goes on, it may be possible to shorten your list of requirements and your circumstances to avoid, becoming more flexible and less tied to oddities in routine that are difficult to maintain on the road. That scenario would be desirable and might result in less worry and fewer complications.

The low-maintenance singer with one bag will probably have many fewer obstacles to overcome to get onstage. But that doesn't necessarily mean one's performance will be better or more memorable than the high-maintenance singer who needs a dolly before getting out of the airport. Rather, it's the knowledge of what you feel you need in order to survive that will be freeing and will allow you to better prepare yourself mentally and physically before a performance. Knowing whether you are high or low maintenance can make a world of difference when planning a career.

* * *

REMINDERS!

- Although it is difficult, an artist can thrive among detractors.
- If isolated artistically, seek support from mentors in your field.
- Experiment with various kinds of artistic expression.
- Find the expressive niche that makes you special.
- Narrow your repertoire and clean out the deadwood.
- Know how needy you are and plan accordingly.

THREE

Tap into a Rhythm

It would be lovely if we could put our performance art in a closet for safekeeping, locked in a velvet-lined box, unaffected by the outside world, rested and ready to be retrieved when we need it. Unfortunately, it goes everywhere we go and is variously pummeled or pampered on a daily basis. Therefore, it is important to develop a mental and physical rhythm to life that will produce an optimum performance when it is expected.

Performers are easily diverted from their goals by self-doubt and worry. Without a positive mental attitude toward making art, the necessary technical skills for performing at a high level are more difficult to achieve, keeping artists from reaching their potential. So, each performer must spend quality time finding ways to establish hope, cheerful expectation, confidence, and constructive thinking as key elements in the development of a career in performance.

ELIMINATE THE NEGATIVE

Negativity is all around us. We hear bad news on television at all hours of the day and night. Our friends confide terrible things that have happened in their lives, and we empathize. Movies and television shows are filled with terror, crime, and people who can't seem to cope with everyday life. There is no way to escape it forever unless you become a hermit, move to the outskirts of civilization, disconnect from all electronic communication, and never talk to anyone else as long as you live. That scenario does not work for a performer. So, another plan has to be hatched. Instead, it is essential to practice focusing more on the positive things in your life than the negative ones, if you want to make an emotional shift in that direction.

It is also important to beware of information overload, which is so prevalent today. The constant texting and obsessive checking of e-mail, Facebook, and Twitter can contribute to depression and frenzy and be too distracting, especially right before a performance or rehearsal or while preparing for those events. Communications such as these should be brought down to a bare minimum right before any performance, since some information might change your positive mood into a negative one and contribute to anxiety when you least want it.

The cultivation of a positive belief system is crucial to success because what we believe about our abilities has a profound effect on those abilities. Innate talent might get a performer started on an illustrious career path, but negative thought patterns or distracting events and conditions may appear along the way to impede success.

Ability is not a fixed property. There is a huge variability in how one performs, due in part to the performer's state of mind during rehearsals and just before taking the stage for an appearance. Nagging negativity that lurks in the mind, waiting for an opportunity to be heard, can derail a performance. If it is allowed a voice, all could be lost.

Those who have a feeling of control over life tend to meet challenges or take advantage of opportunities in terms of how to handle them, rather than worrying about what can go wrong. They feel more centered and calm in the face of turmoil around them. So, changing a negative mindset from *I wonder if I can* to *I know I can* and *What if* to *It will* is a pivotal mental step that must be taken for all performers, especially those who are plagued by doubt. Psychological change doesn't happen overnight; it requires constant repetition of positive mantras and visualization of successful outcomes to squelch obsessive negative thoughts.

I see consequences of the mind's influence on self-confidence in the singers I coach. A lack of confidence can affect performance level in any field of endeavor. But because I teach an audible performance art, I see and hear its effects perhaps more quickly than those in other professions might.

The singing voice is affected by everything we do, everything we eat, and everything we think. Serious vocalists generally forgo late-night parties and stay away from dust, milk products, cigarettes, chocolate, sugary drinks, alcohol, and certain kinds of drugs, even aspirin, because these things can have a negative effect on the quality of the vocal sound, on breathing, allergies, and overall energy. As one of my voice students pointed out, she might as well have become a nun.

Singers must be careful not to talk too much or too loudly, especially on days when they have a performance. I recently heard Celine Dion say in a television interview that she never speaks on days when she is doing her show. She writes down all of her communications. This may be an extreme example, but singers who don't follow a healthy regimen may suffer irreparable harm to their instrument or have a short career, literally "blowing out" the voice in a few years. We have only one voice, and when that one is seriously harmed, it may not be able to be fixed.

So, after reading this, you should not be surprised that singers tend to worry about everything. Emotional upsets immediately affect the voice. Just recall what happens to your voice when you feel sad or angry or perhaps have cried about something: the tone of the voice changes. It becomes scratchy, harsh, or weak. Therefore, it is crucial that singers learn to think positively about all that they do, or the worry and fear of failure will take over; doubts concerning vocal technique and strength will appear; and the voice will disappear. With all of this in mind, it is crucial to take care of oneself in psychological and physical ways, develop tools that rid the mind of worry, and build confidence and enough concentration to sing well despite a multitude of distractions that may be going on around you. It is no easy task, but it can be done.

Performers are often so focused on themselves that they neglect the development of good interpersonal relationships. This void can cause them to become obsessed with their own weaknesses to a fault. The creation of good interpersonal relationships is extremely important when seeking to eliminate negativity from one's life. One of the ways that singers can improve their ability to remain on a positive course is to stay away from negative situations and negative people as much as possible. The old saying that *some people see the glass half empty and others see it half full* is certainly true. It is quite normal to have some of each kind in your life. We all do. But there are some people who seem to see the glass completely empty all of the time. Those are the people who need to be avoided. They tend to make every situation bleak, take all of the excitement out of life, cause everyone around them to feel depressed, and are unable to give any kind of positive support to others.

If there are extremely negative vibes coming from people in your life, causing you to have excessive doubts about your performance possibilities or bringing your self-esteem down to a very low level, then it may be necessary to remove yourself from their presence and seek out other friends and supporters who have a more positive attitude about life and its possibilities. Your spirits will be lifted by a change of emotional environment. That doesn't mean that you only want people around you who praise your every effort, who tell you that everything you do is wonderful (even if it isn't), and who never give you constructive advice. But it does mean that you want to eliminate those who criticize your every move, make you feel less of a person for your thoughts and actions, and never give psychological support to your creative ideas. That kind of atmosphere is not a constructive one. Instead, you need to find supporters, colleagues, and friends who will be there when you are in a pinch, who act as safety nets that will catch you when you fall, help you get through any problems you encounter, be present emotionally, and really listen when you need to talk to someone about an issue that is causing you to worry or feel negative about your future as a performer. Having a confidant like that can get you back on track when feeling down and spur you on to the next step toward achieving your goals.

Certain places have a toxic atmosphere as well. It's almost as if the accumulation of negative attitudes from the people who inhabit them have penetrated the very materials from which they are built. Some workplaces are like that. There is a sense of dread or doom upon entering the building. The same is true for some creative entities. It could be an artist colony, an opera company, a choral group, a musical theatre troupe, a university music department, or another situation in which the performing artist spends a great deal of time. It may be impossible to put into words exactly what has caused this unhealthy atmosphere to exist, but something in the history there has brought about a negative atmosphere that is not conducive to the enjoyment of creative activity. It changes the way that we feel about ourselves, our art, and our surroundings when we experience it, and it can cause artists to become inert, since they are supersensitive people. Sometimes, it is impossible to get away from an environment like this if your educational status or financial situation depends on that entity for support, but alternatives should be found, if at all possible. Otherwise, it may become more and more difficult for the performer to stay positive when worn down by an endemic negativity in the environmental atmosphere.

Another way that performers can eliminate the negative in their lives is to make it a point to seek out humor at every turn, in everything that happens. That is not a natural thing for some people. For others, humor is a part of their normal personality. Whichever the case, if you are feeling negative overload from difficult economic times, heavy performance and rehearsal schedules, a piling-on of criticism, or vocal technique problems that just won't go away, try to break the pattern of negativity by doing something that will make you laugh. Watch only funny movies or videos of your favorite stand-up comedian every day for a week; schedule lunch or coffee with a friend who always sees things on the bright side; and make a list of everything that makes you smile, and make a point to actually smile when you write it down. I've used all of these tactics to zap negative thought patterns, and I found that they really work to put you on a better, healthier road to positive thinking. Sometimes that is difficult to do, but it works and becomes a habit once you make a point to observe and enjoy humor.

DEVELOP A ROUTINE

One way that performers can bolster confidence is by establishing a well-oiled, comforting routine that puts them in optimum vocal, mental, and physical condition. It doesn't matter what that routine involves, how odd it appears, or who agrees with it as long as it works for you. The first thing that a singer must do is develop a vocal warm-up routine that works to get the voice in a smooth, relaxed, focused feeling for the task at hand. There are as many warm-up routines as there are professional singers. Different kinds of exercises and lengths of warm-up work for different people. So, I will not spend time giving you an exact routine to follow. But it must be stressed that without such a plan, it is more likely that the voice will not respond as wished when the performance is in full tilt. Singers are dealing with muscles, thought processes, and reaction time when warming up the voice, much as a tennis player who is preparing to play for the Wimbledon title. I doubt such a player would go out and play never having picked up the racket prior to the match. The primary goal is to literally warm up the voice, not force it or tax it so much that all of the money notes are left in the practice room. The voice should not be tired before the performance begins. If it is, it may never last until the performance is over. So with that in mind, a warm-up routine should be developed that takes the voice just to the edge of being ready to sing as you walk on the stage. This kind of warm-up will add years to your singing life. It is a routine that should be kept for as many years as you wish to sing. You never grow out of it. From personal experience, I can say that the older I get, the more I need to warm up and coax my voice to the point where it agrees to sing as I wish. Also, remember that if you take off several weeks from singing for a vacation or illness, it will take a good bit longer to warm up the voice once you start singing again, until it remembers just what you want it to do.

I feel that it is a good idea to stay in touch with your singing voice every day—with a little humming, soft vocal slides, or perhaps a lilting line or two from your favorite song—even if you are not planning to sing a concert or have a rehearsal right away. That way, the voice is always in shape and can be made ready for a performance rather quickly.

Performers must be careful not to lose all attachment to reality and engage in outrageous and destructive things on performance days. It is not a good time to investigate foods that use spices never tasted previously, try out a new perfume fragrance or hairspray, get a spray tan that might spew strange chemicals into the breathing system, eat half a fried chicken within thirty minutes of the performance, race around all day talking and entertaining friends or family who have come for the performance, or wait until fifteen minutes before the performance to try on your concert dress only to find out that it is too tight and doesn't allow you to take a deep breath. Any of these items could cause the body and voice to react badly. Yet, these kinds of behaviors are common among undisciplined performers.

It's vital to pay attention to how your body reacts to stress—everything you put in it (food, drugs, alcohol) and the physical demands put on it. If the body is out of balance and responds badly to certain stimuli or overwork, a shift must occur in the daily routine to get that body into a satisfactory rhythm for performance. Poor university student singers are often caught between demands from several authority figures for the use of their talent. They may be required to go to a choir rehearsal in the morning (because of an upcoming concert tour) and an opera rehearsal in the afternoon (when they are scheduled to sing a senior recital that evening). If neither of those in charge is willing to allow those singers the rest they need to sing well in the evening, a top-notch performance will be quite difficult to achieve. Those kinds of situations should never happen, but unfortunately they do.

It will take a bit of analysis to figure out which habits are bad for the performance process. But those bad habits must be rooted out, discarded forever, and replaced with ones that soothe the mind and body, preparing them for the ultimate goal: a smooth, seamless, confident presentation. There are several strategies that I have found to help make a performance day go smoother:

1. Warm up the voice gently and just enough to coax it into readiness—but no more.
2. Don't engage in loud talking.
3. Stay away from smoke and dust.
4. Plan a day filled with leisurely things that make you feel relaxed.
5. Warm up the body with breathing exercises and perhaps a little physical exercise but not too much.
6. Be sure to eat. Have a light, nonspicy meal at least two hours before the performance.
7. Don't obsess about the performance by constantly reviewing the music and the words right up until you walk onto the stage.
8. Arrive at the concert hall in plenty of time to get settled and not feel harried.
9. Keep away from hustle and bustle backstage. Find a quiet space to get centered.
10. Concentrate on positive thoughts and stay away from negative people.

When I was a young singer, I didn't know myself very well and spent little time thinking about a daily performance-day routine and how it might affect my singing. But as the pressures of performing started to drain my energy and concentration, I realized that changes needed to be made to be at a peak performance level when required.

When I'm at home on a normal day, I like to wake up quietly about 9 am—though 7 am is more likely on weekdays—with no light coming into the room to shock my brain and with the sound machine softly playing an ebb tide of waves into my right ear while I readjust my body onto the *very* soft pillows under my head. After a few minutes, I raise up a little and squint to see exactly what time it is but fall back on the pillows wishing it wasn't really *that* time already. Then, my right hand reaches toward the nightstand for the TV zapper. Finding the little red button to turn on the *Today Show*, I lie motionless, repeating silently, "This is a wonderful day, I will rejoice and be glad in it." I believe none of it at that point and finally drag myself out of bed, open the blinds, make up the barely mussed bed—since I never move an inch during the night—clear my body of bad energy with a breath-holding, arm-waving exercise I learned from one of my health gurus, and determine to meet the day.

Somehow, I get from there to the breakfast table, where my husband has laid out my morning repast. He's a cheerful morning person who learned early on in our marriage not to ever throw open the bedroom curtains, talk, sing, or make noise before I'm fully awake. Once I've eaten and scanned the paper, I can begin to make somewhat coherent sentences and see that there is a difference between the stove and the kitchen sink. After a very cold shower, a few Callanetics stretches, breathing exercises, and a vocal warm-up of hums and slides while getting dressed, my neurons fire, my blood pressure rises to 90/70, and I get enough energy to meet the day. I have never been a morning person, even as a child, so there is no hope that things might change.

After a good bit of trial and error, I developed a performance-day plan that works well for me. If the event is local, I don't teach students or use my voice very much on those days except to warm up a little in the morning and again in the evening prior to the concert. I follow my usual waking, eating, and exercising routine and spend the day doing normal chores around the house; anything mindless will do. I make sure that I eat food that will not upset my digestion, nothing spicy, my favorites being baked chicken, baked potato, and peas. Bland and benign.

A few hours prior to the concert, I look briefly at the music, close my eyes, and picture walking out onto the stage as the audience applauds; I repeat a positive mantra, such as *I am well prepared*, do an anxiety-reducing breath exercise—four counts breathing in, seven counts holding the breath, and eight counts breathing out (repeated seven times)—and I proceed to get dressed.

Unfortunately, this ritual is difficult to maintain when my performance is away from home. I do have a travel-size sound machine, but no one is there to put food in front of me before I get dressed. My schedule may not allow for desired dallying and pampering. There may be no time for exercising. I may be staying in the room with my accompanist—who tolerates all of my quirks—and some hotels just don't have soft pillows or water that is cold enough to shock me awake. In other words, *I have to get a life!* So does every other performer who has created a pleasurable, effective daily routine that is hard to live without.

To function well when traveling to sing concerts, I make a conscious determination to be flexible and allow for changes to my normal routine. I write out an ideal scheme for the performance day so that I do not feel directionless, making sure that it includes some of my perceived requirements that bring me into peak mental and physical form: time to do stretching, breathing exercises, and tai chi.

I am not a sitter or a napper. The idea of waking up in the morning and waiting all day to sing a concert with nothing to do in between makes me nervous. So, I have to have distractions. If I'm on the road, I invent things to occupy my time. Fortunately, my long-time accompanist, Patsy Wade, and I are much alike. Performance hosts have looked at us as if we were crazy when we asked about the location of the nearest mall. They have dropped us off; we've taken cabs, ridden buses and subways, or walked a few blocks to shopping destinations in towns from Jackson, Mississippi, to Boston, London, and Vancouver, where we browsed, perhaps had lunch, and enjoyed being away from the hotel for a few hours.

After a jaunt such as this, I like to come back to the hotel and rest for a couple of hours, think a little about the music to be sung, do a few breathing and stretching exercises, eat an early dinner—always searching for something fairly bland—warm up quietly as I get dressed, and arrive at the performance hall about thirty minutes before going on the stage. A perfect performance or dress-rehearsal day!

Usually, this kind of routine works well, but there are memorable occasions when the best-laid plans crumbled under the weight of obligations or complications, and none of the above happened. One such event occurred about twenty years ago when I was invited to perform as part of a multiperformer, elaborate—lots of sound and lighting equipment—new music festival in Boston. My portion of the dress rehearsal was scheduled for 6 pm on the evening before the concert. My accompanist, Rosemary Platt, and I had flown in early in the day, eaten a very light lunch, and planned to eat dinner right after the rehearsal, around 7:30. Unfortunately, nothing went as planned.

We arrived at the concert hall at our appointed time to find that the rehearsal schedule had been readjusted without our knowledge, and we were told to wait around to be "worked into" the new schedule in a short while. Other performers continued to rehearse until after 8:30, and we did not get on stage until 9:00.

Neither of us had thought to bring snacks, and there were no restaurants nearby. Besides, we dared not leave, for fear that our rehearsal time would come and go while we were searching for food. It was almost 10:30 when we finally got to a restaurant. By that time, I was exhausted from a very long day, waiting around with nothing to do in an empty concert hall, and I had low energy from too little food and a lingering health issue. It was after midnight when we finally got to the house where we were staying. I didn't fall asleep until 3:30 in the morning, since my brain had been revved up by the rehearsal and the late meal.

It took a lot of rest the next day (I never left my room except to eat), plenty of positive self-talk, and a mental projection of my ability to be in top form for the evening performance. On this occasion, my normal performance-day routine had to be changed. I had slept restlessly and awakened around 10:30 in the morning, having missed breakfast. There was no energy for shopping malls or a leisurely lunch in a local café on this day. Our kind host fixed a light lunch and, later, an early dinner so that we would not have to go out.

When we arrived at the hall an hour or so before the concert, other performers were milling around in the small offstage wing where we had to wait until time to go out onto the stage. Our piece (a dramatic thirty-minute monodrama called *Herstory III: Jehanne de Lorraine*, by Elizabeth Vercoe) was placed near the end of the program, so there was another forty-five-minute wait before going on—a time in which I tried to block out the distractions going on around me by repeating a few mantras, such as *I am well prepared, I have plenty of energy,* and *This will be an excellent performance.* When it was time, I willed myself onto the stage and visualized energy floating around my body (a technique that has become useful to me over the years) and walked toward the lights as a white-tuniced apparition of Joan of Arc.

Amazingly, this turned out to be one of the most successful concerts in our artistic collaboration. We received several curtain calls from the packed house and managed to please the composer who was in attendance. A line from the *Boston Phoenix* review said, "Mabry's voice can evaporate or rise and hang suspended as if over a precipice." That reviewer must have been psychic.

I tried never to let this kind of rehearsal scenario happen to me again. From that day on, I double-checked rehearsal schedules and carried appropriate snacks and water wherever I went. However, no matter how carefully you prepare, there can still be chaos, with little to do but forge onward, knowing that with experience, the power of positive thinking, complete preparation, inner confidence, and a large dose of luck, you can produce a successful outcome.

There have been times when I neglected, for too long a time, the routine that I know works well for me, causing myself great physical and mental distress. One such occasion was about fifteen years ago. At that time, I had a wonderful personal physician who had known me since my late twenties. He was a musician in high school and college, had quite a few musicians as patients, and seemed to understand our psyche. He gave me good advice on many occasions, but one quote remains embedded in my brain.

One day I went to him complaining of feeling worn out, having achy joints and "brain fog," not able to sleep well through the night, and generally in a "blue funk." I had decided that something was terribly wrong. He asked what I'd been doing of late. After describing my full teaching schedule, my university committee commitments, the four concerts I'd just sung in the past month, the travels to New York and Vancouver, and the fact that I had several writing deadlines to make, he leaned back in his chair and said, "I'm surprised you are able to sit here in an upright position and tell me all of this. Now listen, young lady, there are two kinds of horses, plough horses and racehorses. *Artists are racehorses; they are more sensitive to everything.* They scare easily and jump at the slightest motion. They need pampering, tending to, less stress, and regular routines. You are the racehorse. You have to get your routine in order, do less, and stop burning the candle at both ends."

With that, I was dismissed to get blood work and told to come back with a new plan, which I did. I concentrated on reestablishing my old, comfortable routine; I added tai chi, meditation, and relaxation-response breathing exercises; and I have tried to abide by his advice since then, though I must confess that I have not always been successful. Having grown up in a home that equated idleness with slothfulness, I still feel guilty unless I'm actively engaged in some project or trying to solve a problem.

Finding a comforting performance-day routine that worked well for me over the years was instrumental to my success as a performer. I know that it made a great deal of difference in my ability to perform well under normal conditions and under those that involved added stress. So, to all young singers, I encourage you to take a good look at your situation, decide what works best for you, and try to implement a routine as soon as possible to eliminate periods of distress that need not occur in your performing life.

DON'T SPILL THE BEANS

"How do you make it look and sound so easy?" I remember the night a young singer in the audience asked me that just after a performance in Washington, DC, one I had considered canceling due to the fact that I had been sick for more than two weeks. After making the determination that my voice was still there, though my body had little energy, I simply willed myself to get onto the stage and, through practiced thinking and visualization, successfully fooled a packed hall into believing I was in perfect health. I made a point to smile and walk briskly every time I entered and left the stage. When I spoke to the audience about one of the pieces, I determinedly projected my voice with forward placement and energized diction.

Over a thirty-five-year singing career, I have learned that a confident demeanor and Academy Award–level acting are at the top of the list of requirements when embarking on a performing career of any kind. The audience doesn't care if your plane was late, your brother landed in jail the night before and you were his only phone call, or you are currently taking three kinds of antibiotics to recover from some dreadful illness. They have come to be entertained and carried away from such troubles. It isn't likely that they want to be reminded of them while the performance is going on.

Sometimes, it is necessary and wise to cancel an engagement if the result would be a poor-quality performance or vocal cord injury due to singing. But if the choice is made to go forward, it must be done without revealing any illness or dire circumstances that currently occupy the performer's mind. If the performance cannot be accomplished without visible cues of discomfort while on stage, then by all means, cancel.

I suspect that most audience members would be surprised to know how many times a performer has to muster up a major amount of courage to go out on the stage and bring down the house. There is nothing worse for listeners than knowing that the artist is having physical or emotional difficulties. It is unnerving to watch someone struggle to get through the show. The audience begins to feel restless and tense, worry that there will be a terrible outcome, and cease to enjoy the presentation. Some may even leave, thinking the performer is going to bomb before the end is in sight.

Once the commitment is made, a performer must be wary of any psychological need to include the audience in personal thoughts of doubt that the show will go on as planned. Just stating those doubts aloud or purposely displaying physical or mental distress to get sympathy from the audience is often enough sabotage to cause the outcome to be less than pleasant for everyone.

* * *

REMINDERS!

- Develop a positive belief system to enhance performance ability.
- Find humor in everything possible.
- Stay away from negative people and situations.
- Practice positive self-talk or mantras to help rid the mind of worry.
- Establish a well-oiled, comforting performance-day routine.
- Notice how your body reacts to stress, things you ingest, and distractions.
- Have a backup plan when your ideal routine is interrupted.
- Don't let the audience know your troubles.

FOUR

It's a Small World

The performing world is an exciting realm and a small one, getting even smaller with the proliferation of the World Wide Web in all of its forms. It is amazing how frequently and easily artists can come into contact with someone for whom they have auditioned, worked, or performed. There are positive and negative aspects to having an almost immediate connection to the world's stage. The artist's past choices, whether good or bad, may be roaming around in cyberspace for all to see. That less-than-stellar performance that a singer wishes to erase from his or her mind may have been recorded on someone's cell phone and put on YouTube. So, it is more acute than ever to make the right choices for repertoire and performance venues to present oneself in the most positive light. You never know what will be remembered as being the standard of your performance abilities.

It's very easy for a young artist to get caught up in the trappings and hype of such a public profession. The psyche can become addicted to the applause, glittery costumes, parties, interviews, autograph signings, and fan fawning. Just being a part of the noise and changeable climate can cause distractions that might derail a promising career. Without careful planning, guidance, and support, the performer may lose track of ultimate goals, make poor choices, develop bad habits in technique, and acquire personality characteristics that cause negative reactions from colleagues and the public.

WHAT NOT TO PERFORM

The choice of appropriate, fulfilling, and engaging repertoire is critical to the development of a successful performance career. Perhaps the most important thing that a performer should focus on in this regard is the acquisition of curiosity—enough curiosity to personally investigate a multitude of repertoire options and not settle for a limited number of pieces and only certain composers or musical styles that have been suggested by others. Also, to stay out of vocal trouble, every performance opportunity's repertoire requirements should be evaluated thoroughly before engagements are accepted.

Young artists accept professional engagements for all kinds of reasons, with monetary needs and an opportunity for public exposure being high on the list. Unfortunately, some singers accept jobs for no good reason at all, except an uneasy need to stay in the public eye as much as possible for fear that one's career will be over otherwise. If a singer selects repertoire and accepts performance opportunities for those reasons alone or to fulfill some obligation to a friend, manager, or teacher without thoughts of repertoire development, problems can occur. This approach might waste precious time that could be used to prepare more significant works that would improve technique, present aspects of the artist's unique talent in a more flattering light, or develop creativity and lend energy to the psyche.

Finally, singers often bow to pressure from handlers or hiring entities to perform works that may negatively affect their career longevity. No one benefits from programming pieces or taking on operatic and musical theatre roles that are much too difficult for current skills or have requirements that might stress or permanently injure the voice. In this case, both the performer and the audience will notice the struggle going on during the performance, and the residual effects to the voice and career may be difficult to overcome.

Every performer can benefit from multiple repetitions of any given work. But a lack of variety in repertoire that excites the imagination or slightly stretches existing technical and musical abilities can be stifling for the artist. If repertoire is geared mostly toward the supply-and-demand point of view, artistic development may stall, and technical ability could level off or decrease from a lack of challenge.

The memory of the last time that I sang the mezzo-soprano solos in Handel's *Messiah* still makes me smile. It took place about twenty-five years ago in a sold-out performance of more than fifteen hundred people, who had purchased tickets well in advance since the event was a tradition in this particular venue. The concert was being broadcast on public television, and the excitement among the chorus and orchestra was palpable.

I had accepted the engagement several months before but thought little about it as the date approached, except to make my flight reservations and decide what to wear. After all, I had performed these solos many times in the ten years prior, knew them by heart, and secretly wished that Handel had developed writer's block before inking them. As many lyric mezzos like myself will attest, these well-known arias rarely allow the voice to rise above the middle range and are better suited to the heavier, darker mezzo voices or countertenors. However, lighter-voiced mezzos are often engaged to sing them for lack of a better available choice, and there is that monetary consideration for the singer. So, we acquiesce.

Though I had sung my share of Baroque music since student days, I never felt any real connection to it, believing that, as one of my pianist friends put it, there are only two composers in hell—Handel and Vivaldi—doomed to listen to each other's music for eternity. Thus, I did not accept these engagements out of love for the pieces but rather because I wanted to have exposure to the public early in my career. The pieces did not hurt my voice in any way, but there was nothing about them that showed it off to a particular advantage either.

So on this occasion, I sat on the stage among what appeared to be a group of enthusiastic performers and an eager audience; I watched the conductor chew gum (he must have been bored also) as the tenor wafted to his high notes; and I waited for my time to sing, thinking about what I was going to do when the concert was over. I made a mental list of foods to serve at an upcoming party at my house, reviewed details about another concert two weeks off, and wondered if my husband had remembered to feed the dog. In other words, I was simply phoning this performance in, something that appalled me when I realized how unengaged I was. So, I redoubled efforts to connect with the music and concentrated on energizing my singing as the orchestra played the introduction to my next aria. However, as I walked off the stage at the end of the concert with the other soloists to thunderous applause and three curtain calls, I vowed never to sing these pieces again. They and I deserved better.

I learned this good lesson about monotony fairly early in my career and tried not to repeat it as I matured as an artist. The shelf life of repertoire is different for each person. Some can tolerate, even require, endless repetitions of works and still feel the excitement of the first attempt. I discovered that I needed considerable variety in performance repertoire to keep the excitement and enthusiasm in my performances. It is important for each performer to be aware of personal preferences in this regard and notice when stale air creeps into rehearsals or performances. Too much sameness in repertoire choices or excessive repetition can lead to boredom and lackluster performances.

Sometimes the thrill of being chosen to perform for a particular occasion seems to mangle all connections in the artist's brain. Inexperienced performers are more likely to say "yes" without thoroughly investigating all aspects of the engagement than are those who have been on the circuit for a while—but veterans are not immune to regret. Premieres of new works fall into that category. They are exciting, enticing, publicity-producing events. They can generate reviews and large crowds, bring out influential people in the profession, and promise exposure difficult to come by for some artists. Sometimes a career can be catapulted into high gear if the outcome is successful. So, it is tempting to jump at the chance to be part of such an experience.

Some performers covet participation in milestones like this so much that they don't pay enough attention to exactly what it is they have been contracted to sing. In some cases, they commit without ever having looked at the music. This can be a fatal mistake if the piece turns out to be unsuited to the voice type, weight, and color and too difficult for its current technical level or too musically complex, or the performer simply hates it and finds it a chore to learn when faced with reality. In either scenario, the performance is probably doomed to mediocrity, and the whole experience will be less than satisfactory.

I can relate to the joy and electricity surrounding premieres, having sung more than thirty in my career. They are powerful vehicles for expression. The idea that you are the first person to perform a work in public, setting the standard for all of those who come after you, is quite heady, perhaps too much so. The kick of it can cause one to make bad choices.

Most of those events are colorful, happy memories for me, but there were a couple of occasions when I regretted having accepted invitations to sing premieres. In each case, there was a good bit of agony involved in the rehearsal process since neither my accompanist nor I ever felt a connection to the music. We had to rely heavily on our experience and professionalism and determine to put a positive light on every aspect of the preparation and execution to get through it.

Once the decision has been made to accept a premiere, it is important to give no clues of dissatisfaction to those involved in the event, especially the composer of the work. Casting a pall over the proceedings would only leave a bad impression and erase further opportunities for performance in that venue. Though both events had good outcomes, I was relieved when the performances were over, and I never programmed the works again. Unless there is a requirement in your contract to repeat the work, this is a choice that can be made by the performer.

It is easy to get caught up in the expectation of a lofty, glittery premiere and forget what it might take to make the piece work for your instrument and musical personality. Sometimes, especially with new music, an inordinate number of rehearsals required to stage it could prove daunting and take precious hours needed to rehearse for other upcoming engagements, causing anxiety at having too little time to prepare for either.

Every artist needs to ask a number of questions before accepting an invitation to sing a premiere. First and foremost, *Do I like the music? What does the music do for me: emotionally, musically, vocally? What special qualities can I bring to the music? Do I have time to learn the music? Will I be compen-*

sated and does that matter? If there are no positive answers to any of these questions, then perhaps it is best to let another person have the opportunity.

If the answers to those questions are positive, then other questions must be considered: *How many rehearsals will be needed, and have they been scheduled and organized well? Does the instrumentation and concert setting suit the size of my voice? Are the other performers capable musicians?* Again, negative responses to these questions may provide reasons to decline if the outcome seems dubious. Therefore, careful thought and consideration should be taken before agreeing to perform any work, no matter how important the occasion. To do otherwise could spell disaster.

WHAT NOT TO WEAR

There are three occasions that make me laugh when I think of personal concert attire. The first one occurred at a guest recital I performed for a national convention of voice teachers. Following the concert, Patsy and I were enjoying comments from people in a long receiving line when suddenly an attractive, vibrantly dressed woman appeared in front of me, reached around my neck, took hold of the top back of my black long-sleeved beaded gown, pulled it up sharply to see the label, and said, "I've got to know who designed that dress. Just love it!" Seeing the name, she exclaimed, "I knew it. I have to know where you got it!" Caught completely off guard, I mumbled something about Philadelphia, glimpsed the shocked look on several faces in line, just smiled, and tried to change the subject. I'm glad to say that has never happened since. I hope she liked the concert.

The second occasion was a recital given for a regional National Association of Teachers of Singing convention in Arkansas. At the end of the concert, I was greeting members of the audience when two smiling, nattily dressed young men came running forward. After making generous comments about the performance, one asked if he could take my picture and added, "Could we see your rings? They look fabulous from the audience. We couldn't keep our eyes off them." Apparently, the anniversary gift from my husband had been caught in the lights. When I told him the story he laughed and said, "Those lights must have had magnifiers on them."

The third and most bizarre episode followed a performance for a convention of advertisers and business people on a cold night in February in a newly refurbished historic train station lobby with towering light fixtures and huge plants surrounding the stage. I was performing musical theatre pieces and light pop standards with a small instrumental ensemble and two other singers. We all donned our most glittery outfits for the occasion. Mine was a spectacular red-sequined dress—one that I bought in New Orleans and wore for several concerts of various types—that prompted a flamboyant woman at a reception in South Carolina to grab my arm and say, "Honey, I'd like to rip that dress right off you." It fit like a glove, had a side zipper, and had to be pulled on over my head and off the same way. I could put it on by myself, but there was no way I could get it off without help. It took another person—usually Patsy—to pull it off me, one arm at a time, while I was leaning over with my head nearly touching the floor. I'm surprised she didn't write this duty into her contract. On one road trip, it got stuck in midextraction and we danced around the room several times, pulling and wriggling—laughing the whole time—trying to find just the right contortion that would allow it to slip off over my head. On this occasion, the train station was packed, and the audience seemed to love the program. Apparently, the red dress made a fashion statement once more when, at the end of the show, a bejeweled woman with flaming red hair came up to me, introduced herself, and said, "That is the most fabulous dress you have on. It really glows under the lights. What you need is a nice fur coat to go with it. If you'll come out to my car, I have one in my trunk that I want you to try on. I'll sell it to you for a really cheap price." That was an offer I decided to decline.

We're being watched every second we are onstage, studied from head to toe, every detail of our facade analyzed by the audience, staring in our direction. So, careful thought must be given to dressing appropriately when on exhibition. When it comes to dressing for success in the classical music genre, it is truly a man's world. Male singers and instrumentalists have little to worry about when thinking about what to wear while performing. They can manage dozens of concerts with a well-fitted black tuxedo, complete with all the trappings; a nicely tailored suit and crisp white shirt and tasteful tie; and one additional black outfit in a more casual vein, perhaps a black turtleneck or Nehru shirt with black pants and black shoes. If they wore those three outfits for forty years, no one would notice or complain.

However, female performers, especially singers and pianists, live in another universe. Several years ago, I was invited to present a recital at the Southern Baptist Theological Seminary in Louisville, Kentucky. A large enthusiastic crowd had turned out for my rather traditional recital that included German lieder, French mélodie, and American art songs. At the reception following the performance, I was pleased to hear numerous comments about what had been performed, including joy at the programming of a few unfamiliar works. However, one comment was priceless. A lively young man, effusive in his accolades, shook my hand vigorously and said, "When I decided to come to this concert, I didn't know that I had heard you sing before. But I knew I was in for a treat when I saw your accompanist come onto the stage. I remembered your terrific concert at Tennessee Technological University when I was an undergraduate. Your accompanist had on the same dress." Though it was a lovely, light pink satin dress made especially for her, she was not amused, having overheard his comment. She never wore it again in my presence. That kind of comment would never be made about a male performer—thus, the female dilemma.

There are crucial decisions to be made when deciding what to wear for auditions and performances. In the ideal world, every artist would have a keen sense of fashion and instinctively know what to wear for every occasion. Indeed, there are people blessed with that gift. But for many, understanding which fashion styles, colors, and dress lengths are suited to their physique and performance needs falls into the category of understanding a foreign language. Thus, choosing an appropriate wardrobe required by the profession becomes a challenge.

Singers need good professional advice from people who know exactly what is expected for a classical performance venue. This is where many young performers go astray when trying on clothes. They seek advice only from store clerks, who may be working on commission, or from family members and friends, who may not have a good sense of style or understand the artist's professional needs.

Again, male singers have fewer details to think about once they have those three outfits mentioned earlier. The primary error that jumps out when a male performer takes the stage is the proper fit of the clothing he chooses to wear.

I used to live in a house that had a whole wall of mirrors that went from the ceiling to the baseboard on the left as you entered the front door. One afternoon, one of my male students came to the house for the first time. He was six feet three inches tall. Upon entering, he looked left, saw himself in the mirrors, and stood fixated for several minutes admiring his visage. He turned to me and said, "I've never seen my whole body in a mirror before. This is really cool." I have a feeling that is more common than we might suspect, given the lack of attention that some male performers pay to length of pants, jackets, and jacket sleeves.

I have a voice-teacher friend who sends her male students once a year to get their dress pants and jackets tailored to just the right fit and length. Then, each is required to parade across the stage in full regalia to make sure that shirt collars are not too tight, suit jackets are not too big or too small, sleeves are hemmed to the proper length, and there is no pooling of fabric around the tops of shoes nor inches of socks visibly appearing below the pants and atop the shoes. She, like I, has seen ill-fitting clothing one too many times on the concert stage and knows that it is distracting and difficult to focus on the sound of the voice when the body housing it looks uncomfortable in its clothes. Therefore, before embarking on any auditions or concert engagements, every male singer needs to find a good tailor at a department store or small business and have all professional attire altered to fit.

A performer may not remain at the same weight and wear the same size forever. If there happens to be a dramatic weight gain or loss, then adjustments must be made or new clothes purchased so that they still have an easy fit. I recall being in the audience when a young, upcoming tenor was singing a guest performance at my university. His voice was glorious, and the music was well presented in style and interpretation. However, these fine qualities were overlooked by some in the audience because his neck was bulging over his shirt collar, making one wonder if he might choke; his tuxedo jacket was also at least a size too small (perhaps two), and his pants were so long that he could have cut three inches and been at the right length. At intermission, all one heard in the lobby was conversation about his appearance, not his singing. Such a shame! I'm sure that he would have been surprised to hear those comments. This kind of scenario is easily avoided with guidance by professionals. So, every male singer must seek out a good tailor and keep up-to-date with alterations.

Females have numerous decisions to make when choosing what to wear for auditions and performances. Fortunately, there are plenty of sources for information to help with the answers, such as the *Classical Singer* periodical and books such as those listed at the back of this volume. But having taught a lot of singers and watched as they agonized over what to wear, I have observed a multitude of sins occur when faced with this dilemma. I'd like to point out a few mistakes that seem to be recurring themes in attire choices—choices that can change the atmosphere of any performance situation.

Do not wear gownless evening straps, dangling jewelry, shawls, or dresses with slits up to the wah-hoo! That was the directive given by my undergraduate university choral director when she advised her all-female choir about appropriate dresses for the spring concert. We all knew what she meant. It is distracting and embarrassing to watch singers pull up sliding strapless dresses between songs, prominently display knees that peer out from a long slit in the front of a dress, continuously retrieve a shawl that has slid off the shoulders every few bars, or clank on and off the stage with large noisy bangles dangling from ears, neck, and wrists. It isn't necessary to cover up in a nunlike fashion when onstage. However, showing too much skin, creating major distractions with jewelry, or wearing a dress that causes the audience to fear that some part of it might actually fall off during the concert is not an optimum scenario either. And nothing is uglier than knees on the stage. Also, one has to consider the fabric when choosing a dress that will be presented in harsh or reflected light from the back of the stage. If the material is flimsy or see-through, not only may it have no particular shape that flatters the singer's body, but it may also be possible to see more than the singer wants to reveal to the audience, especially if she is ignorant of this problem and doesn't wear appropriate undergarments. So, unless you perform in a musical genre where anything goes, a la Lady Gaga, whose costume is part of the performance, discretion is key when choosing concert attire, especially for classical venues.

It is important to know what colors bring out your best features and complement your eyes, complexion, and hair color under all kinds of lighting: stage, artificial, and natural. Auditions and performances can occur under any of those lighting conditions, so it is important to have clothes in colors that work for each. Some people look wonderful in pale pink or lavender, but if I wore either, someone in the audience might call an ambulance since I would appear washed out, as if I might expire before the concert was over. White is another difficult color to wear on-stage. It can make us look larger than we are, and it can drain the features of definition unless one has black hair and eyes. I discovered early on that rich colors or black look best on me, and I have not strayed from that palette.

"Am I a summer, winter, fall, or spring?" asked one of my students as she contemplated going shopping for her senior recital dress. Answering her own question, she continued, "I think I'm a fall. My favorite color is brown." Unfortunately for her, brown and other dull colors are not optimum choices for performing under lights unless the material is shiny and the lights are bright. She was referring to color palette shopping according to complexion and hair color, which has become popular over the past few years. It's a useful approach, but one needs guidance from someone versed in its complexities, before slogging through a department store willy-nilly with a color chart in hand, trying on anything that looks like it might fit a particular category. That could prove frustrating and take forever. Each singer must spend time investigating, with professional help, where she fits on the color chart so that shopping for professional attire will go faster and be more productive, thus immediately eliminating all possibilities that do not fall into the ideal color spectrum.

It doesn't matter how beautiful the dress is if it doesn't fit or the style does not suit your figure. I am height challenged, being five feet three inches tall. So, my first goal in choosing attire for any occasion is finding something with a design that makes me look taller—usually solid colors, no large patterns, and few if any frills. I'm a more clean-lined, classic kind of person. A singer who is five feet ten inches tall with a flamboyant personality might have other considerations. Each singer needs to realistically assess which physical elements and personality traits she wishes to accent and which to de-emphasize in her stage wardrobe because, once onstage, things get magnified in ways that a singer does not always desire—especially dizzying dress patterns, poor color choices, and styles that do not flatter the performer's body.

Accidents can happen to any piece of attire that you choose to wear in concert: a heel can break or fall off a shoe; seams can rip apart; the hem of a dress can suddenly decide to unravel; stockings can get a run in them.

When I travel for concerts, I always take an extra pair of shoes, stockings, and a small thread-and-needle repair kit, just in case, and my accompanist always carries scotch tape, which she used on two occasions to fix my hem when it decided to unravel backstage before the concert. There are more secure ways to fix hems than that. Just visit your local cloth store for suggestions from those who know all the tricks.

Finally, it is imperative that any newly purchased concert attire receive a trial run before the actual event. All of it should be bought and tried on together so that you are certain that all elements work together. Don't make any assumptions or last-minute changes that have not been thought through completely. Also, it is best if store personnel can do alterations, if they offer that service. They are inclined to get hems even and make the finished product look professional, more so than your Aunt Martha, who may have never worked with such a fancy dress material.

Unfortunately, with inexperienced performers, the first time that a concert dress is worn will be the concert for which it was bought, and accessories will be added without much thought as to how they feel or how they fit the rest of the outfit. Many things could have changed since you purchased the dress, perhaps several months before. Weight can change dramatically over a short period, and the shoes you've planned to wear may not be the right heel height for the dress length, since they were not bought at the same time and never tried on with the dress—thus, surprises: the dress is too tight in the waist to take a really good breath, it lacks two inches meeting in the back, and has to be covered with a jacket or laced up with ribbons at the last minute; or it is too long to walk easily in it without holding up the front; or the new, never-worn five-inch heels are impossible to walk in, causing the singer to hobble on- and offstage due to incredible pain in the toes; and the huge red rose pinned impulsively at the waistline right over the belly button exhales and inhales every time the singer does so that the audience is drawn to it like a magnet. It doesn't matter how beautiful the clothes are if you can't sing or walk in them or they detract from the performance. So, keep in mind when purchasing concert attire that the total fashion picture, good planning, practicality, and comfort are as important as attractiveness.

WHAT NOT TO SAY

Singing is a subjective art. There is nothing scientific or exact about how listeners perceive it. The sound produced by any given singer may not be universally loved. This applies to performers who have developed successful careers and those who have not. Some listeners may dislike a singer's voice immensely, while others adore it. Since the voice is such a personal instrument, singers are prone to focus too much on criticism or rejection and lose perspective about the mercurial aspects of the performing world.

A singer who goes into this profession with the attitude that the performing world is fair and democratic and the most talented person always comes out on top is naïve and doomed to despair. Even the best performers are not likely to win or be chosen all of the time or even part of the time, because no two audition situations are alike, having different goals and judges who are subjective in their approach to decision making. That is quite obvious when watching some of the reality shows, such as *American Idol* or *America's Got Talent*. No two judges are looking for exactly the same thing in a performer. At times, the judges are not particularly helpful in expressing what they want to see and hear, making it difficult for a performer to glean useful information that might improve the performance. Judges may even disagree about the singer's strengths and weaknesses and give conflicting opinions about the singer's performance, thus creating confusion.

This reminds me of the written observations of three judges I sang for in a regional National Association of Teachers of Singing audition many years ago when I was declared a winner in the graduate division. They all had good, positive, constructive things to say, but one line in each critique provides comedic relief and realism about auditions. The first judge wrote, "Your vibrato is a little fast, try to slow it down a tad." The second penned, "Your vibrato is a bit slow, try to speed it up a little." And the third finished his comments with "One of the things I like most is your vibrato. It is perfect, not too slow, not too fast." When I showed the judges' sheets to my teacher, he laughed and asked, "May I make a copy of these to show to all of my students who obsess about judges' comments?"

These comments have provided a great teaching lesson for my students over the years as well, since it is a perfect example of how three people can sit in the same room at the same time and hear three different things. Though a performer may know this intellectually, it is still a challenge to stop obsessing about criticism. So, each performer must work hard to develop a positive, realistic attitude toward auditions to survive them and not take them personally.

Since we've established that life is not fair, that it is impossible to please everyone, and that things don't always go our way, we must decide as performers how to respond to that reality. When performers personalize auditions and interviews, bad things can happen. To lash out or become confrontational in person or in writing adds nothing constructive to career planning.

Is anything really confidential anymore, or has discretion died a horrible death? It seems that for some people, the primary purpose in life is to display every aspect of their existence to the universe or vent to anyone who will listen. Reality shows, social networking, and neglected etiquette have contributed to a monumental tongue-loosening virus that has taken hold around the world. Unfortunately, it has infected the daily interactions of some performers who rip off vile, sometimes career-damaging tweets, e-mails, and texts that they would surely think twice about saying in person. Public expression of negative reactions to auditions, interviewers, teachers, conductors, or others who might employ a singer can spread a dark cloud over the performer's future. Harsh words spoken in haste might be accidentally overheard by their subject or someone who may know the person.

A few years ago, I was one of three judges listening to auditions for a district Metropolitan Opera audition. The judges agonized over who should win, since several singers presented outstanding performances. At the end of deliberations, winners and alternates were announced from the stage. One of the judges and I headed for the ladies' room before going to the reception, where all the competitors would be given the opportunity to talk with the judges. We were alone in our little cells at first and the room was quiet, but suddenly the bathroom door flung open and two singers came in, one complaining rather loudly about the auditions: how they were run, the ridiculous choice of one of the judges who obviously did not know anything about the repertoire, and how the final decision was ludicrous since she should have won. Unfortunately for her, the judge about whom she was speaking was in the stall next to me, a major surprise to the singer when the stall door opened and she came face-to-face with the judge. It was an awkward moment to say the least. The singer never apologized, just stomped out. The judge looked at me and said, "And she's the one I was promoting to be the winner. I won't ever do that again." Not only did that singer ruin any chance to be reviewed by this judge favorably in some future audition, but it is also likely that the judge told the story to everyone she knew, causing people with whom this singer might come into contact to have already developed a negative opinion about her.

This kind of behavior is not new to the performance profession. The need to gossip, lash out, or take revenge has probably been a staple of the profession since its inception. It just took other forms: the backstage whispers about competitors, whiny notes passed during auditions, grumbling messages left on answering machines, or letters and public comments of complaint to judges at not having been chosen for one thing or another.

Performers should be constantly aware that everything they say might be heard and repeated and that everything they write in cyberspace is doomed to live for eternity. Many are naïve and seem surprised when their negative words about someone or something professional have been found by an employer, coworker, or friend and caused problems for them.

It is important to leave the best impression possible whether you get chosen or not. I am reminded of an occasion when a certain soprano auditioned for the solos in a professional performance of an oratorio. Though she was a fabulous performer, someone else was chosen. She was a good person at heart but unfortunately forgot her manners during the first of three performances. As a paid member of the chorus, she sat onstage behind the soloist during the performance and made faces and derogatory comments to singers on either side of her about the singer who was chosen. This behavior was viewed by the audience and members of the chorus and relayed to the conductor, who had no option but to remove her from her paid position with the chorus. This situation caused problems for the singer's reputation and could easily have been avoided.

Here are a few tips that will help to make an audition and its aftermath a more positive event:

   Try to make friends, not enemies, of those you encounter at auditions and performances.
   Write a thank-you note, rather than threatening or complaining letters, to people for whom you've auditioned—you may see them again.
   Be careful what you say in bathrooms, hallways, and on telephones—you don't know who is listening.
   Don't be demanding and act as if you are different from the others auditioning and deserve special treatment—the "I'm over here" attitude doesn't fare well in the real world.
   Don't exaggerate or lie about your credentials to judges or those around you—you will be found out.
   Treat staff accompanists and backstage workers with the respect they deserve—they can be tremendous help in presenting a good performance.
   Accept the outcome with grace and move on. There will be many more opportunities to showcase your talent.

There are times when a performer must go on with the show under difficult circumstances. An audition may be poorly organized, causing unneeded anxiety for the auditionees. Most performers have also experienced discomfort due to problems with a performance venue; it might be much too cold, much too hot, or have other issues that cause distress.

Two such cases stand out as challenges during my concert career. The first was a guest artist recital for a spring music festival in Iowa. The performance venue was a beautiful, acoustically perfect wooden chapel. However, I wore a long-sleeved, beaded red dress that looked great onstage but became a nightmare in the humid ninety-five-degree afternoon heat. Unfortunately, the auditorium had no air-conditioning. It never occurred to me to ask about that when I agreed to the concert. Everyone in the audience had brought fans that waved rhythmically through the entire concert. I wished for one. The windows were open, but there was no breeze, so my accompanist and I nearly fainted before it was all over. My dress felt heavy and oppressive and was clinging wet from top to bottom, and her hands fairly slid off the wet keys as we ended the concert.

The second event presented an opposite problem. I was singing a guest recital at a university in Virginia in March where the weather had turned unusually cold just before we arrived. Having checked out the weather forecast, I was prepared and took a short fur coat that was perfect for temperatures in the thirties. However, I didn't know until the rehearsal on the morning of the concert that the heating in the concert hall was malfunctioning. It was about fifty-five degrees in the hall when we went to rehearse, but we were assured that by the evening it would be fixed. I'm quite sure the host tried every way possible to get that heating system repaired, but it just didn't happen. So by the time we arrived for the concert, it seemed even colder than earlier in the day. But the show had to go on. There was a large audience, all sitting in fur coats, hats, and gloves waiting to be entertained. We performed the entire recital in temperatures that the voice and fingers hate. This time, I was happy to have on a long-sleeved gown that was rather heavy, but I had to take a break at every natural division in the concert possible and stand backstage in my fur coat with gloves on for a few minutes just to keep going. Patsy did the same. Her hands were so cold that it was challenge to manipulate the ice-cube keys.

I could have complained, thrown a fit, decided not to sing, and created chaos for the venue. But I decided to go on in spite of the problems. I knew there was nothing that could be done about the condition, so no need to multiply the agony for everyone involved. I never complained about the heat or the cold to the audience in either case; I merely thanked them for braving the elements, which brought laughter in the "misery loves company" performances. Later, at the receptions, several people mentioned their appreciation of my lack of complaint. In my experience, I feel that if you decide to go on with the performance, don't complain about the conditions of the audition or performance venue—just try to change what you can, move on, and cope with it.

* * *

REMINDERS!

- The choice of appropriate, fulfilling, and engaging repertoire is critical to career development.
- Don't sing pieces that are too difficult for current skills or that might stress or permanently injure the voice.
- Too much sameness in repertoire can lead to boredom.
- Assess all performance opportunities carefully before accepting engagements, no matter how important the occasion.

- Get professional advice about style, color, and fit of performance attire.
- Practicality, appropriateness, and comfort are as important as attractiveness in concert attire.
- Be sure to practice performing in your new clothes before the performance date.
- Remember that singing is a subjective art and that no two people like the same kinds of sounds or performance personalities.
- Develop a positive, realistic attitude toward auditions.
- Don't lash out when not chosen—move on.
- Be careful what you say or write. It may come back to haunt you.
- Don't complain about what can't be changed with auditions and performance venues. Just try to cope.

FIVE

Project Your Best Self

"That singer has a terrible reputation. She never knows her part, always has excuses, and doesn't show up on time for rehearsals," remarked a renowned conductor when speaking about a singer with whom he had worked. No performer should be pleased to have those words spoken about her. Perfection is a fleeting thing, but all serious performers in any genre should strive to present themselves in a way that causes colleagues and employers to expound about their exemplary reputation, not complain about faults.

It is impossible to go through every day without a miscue here and there. Occasional snafus are easily forgiven. But eventually, an artist's overall professional behavior and preparedness will gain unwanted negative attention when it is less than stellar. This applies to not only musical preparation but also how one presents oneself in front of an audience. Professional stage etiquette is incredibly important. All eyes are on you as you sit or stand on the stage. It doesn't matter whether you are actively singing at the time or not. You are still being watched.

I recently attended a performance that included several seasoned soloists, and I was surprised, along with others in the audience, with the demeanor of two of them. One sang her solos with confidence and lovely tone, then sat down, leaned back in her chair, closed her eyes, and stretched her feet out in front of her, occasionally wiggling her toes, as if she was in her living room watching television, no longer part of the performance. At one point, she pulled out the front neck of her dress as if to make sure everything was still in its place. Later in the performance, one of the male soloists rose to sing one of his arias as the chorus finished one of its sections of the oratorio. He turned his back to the audience to look at the chorus, and he proceeded to push his coat out of the way to scratch his back for several minutes while watching them sing until his entrance. The concert behavior of both singers was distracting at best and noticed by many, as I discovered on a trip to the ladies room at intermission. I overheard several comments about how bored the mezzo seemed, and one woman standing in line asked, "Do you think that tenor has fleas or what?" I doubt that either singer would want to be remembered that way.

KNOW YOUR STUFF

The development of a successful and sustainable performance career depends largely on ultimate preparation. Extensive attention to details is essential but often neglected by young performers. They frequently underestimate the amount of rehearsal time required to bring performance skills to a high level, are surprised when the outcome falls short of expectations, and resort to a multitude of excuses when confronted with reality. Overlearning musical materials is a must to build confidence, promote collegiality with other musicians, and lessen the impact of factors such as anxiety and outside distractions that can sabotage musical expression and concentration.

Excuses are never appropriate in a professional environment. No one wants to hear them. In a practical sense, not knowing the material can get you fired and replaced at a moment's notice, especially in a professional venue. The conductor of a major symphony chorus told me of an incredible incident in which a professional-level soprano, one who had been engaged to sing the solo parts in Stravinsky's *Les Noces* for the regular-season subscription series, called him two weeks before the performance to inquire about how the rehearsals were going. He was alarmed when she asked how he and the chorus were mastering it, remarked that rhythm was not her thing, and asked if he would have his accompanist record the piano part and send it to her so she could learn it. It was obvious that she had accepted the engagement without knowing the piece or understanding how difficult it would be for her to learn. Her management was called the next day, and she was replaced with someone who arrived at the first rehearsal prepared and who subsequently astounded everyone, including the reviewer, with a magnificent rendition of this most difficult piece. Unfortunately, this scenario has happened in other professional settings with symphony orchestras, choruses, and chamber ensembles, and when it does, the unprepared performer must realize that there is always someone "waiting in the wings," tuned up and ready to make his or her mark.

There is no doubt that when some singers arrive unprepared for auditions and rehearsals, it gives all singers a bad reputation until proven otherwise. On more than one occasion, instrumentalists or conductors with whom I performed have complimented me for being well prepared.

They seemed delightedly surprised. I thought that quite odd and couldn't imagine the fear at arriving to rehearse without knowing my part. Apparently, others have done so.

The first time I was engaged to sing George Crumb's *Ancient Voices of Children* (a landmark, exotic, atmospheric, and difficult piece), I had studied the score for weeks, dissected every musical gesture, used segments of the score as vocal warm-ups, memorized large sections (though I would be using music for the performance), listened to Jan De Gaetani's remarkable recording of the work numerous times, and made sure that every hard-to-find pitch was in place. I felt confident that I could hold my own in the rehearsal.

Upon entering the performance hall, I greeted the other musicians, only one of whom I had known previously, and met the Lincoln Center–based conductor for the first time, who asked if I needed to go through any of my part before the whole group began to rehearse. I said no, and we launched into the rehearsal, which ran so beautifully that we finished ahead of schedule. We all expressed excitement about the upcoming performance and joy at the smoothness of the rehearsal, which prompted one instrumentalist to say to me, "Wow, I'm impressed. I can't believe you already knew your part. I thought we'd have to teach you the notes." I just laughed and said, "I'd have sent someone else to sing it if I didn't know the notes." Obviously, he'd acquired a bad impression of singers from past experience.

As a teacher of young singers and a coach for professionals, I have noticed that some have never developed an efficient, practical approach to the learning of repertoire, relying on rote learning or others to teach them the basics at the last minute. This approach is normal for beginners, but as a performer ascends to the semiprofessional and professional ranks, especially for classical singers, more is demanded. Therefore, those hoping to excel in this field must sharpen their practice skills to a level where they feel independent, needing little help in musical preparation. This is especially true for those interested in singing contemporary classical music that has few if any recorded examples for musical direction.

I began music making as a pianist and still accompany singers during lessons, so I feel a keen kinesthetic connection to pitch through my hands on the keyboard. It is the tool that I use to learn new vocal music. I play it first until the shape of the music is embedded in my body; then I begin to sing the vocal line without playing the notes, revisiting them at the keyboard if I make mistakes. Eventually, I discard the playing of my line altogether, concentrating only on the accompanying figures being played around what I'm singing. I believe that this kinesthetic connection to an instrument is very helpful to singers, especially beginners, in developing good relative pitch and a feeling for intervallic relationships. I encourage all singers with whom I work to upgrade their piano skills, and I have found that many improve sight-reading almost immediately when they try this approach.

For those singers who have no piano skills, find them to be a challenge, or need additional help learning music, a pedagogical system such as *solfeggio*, in which each note of the score is sung to a special syllable, is a wonderful way to become proficient at sight-reading and learning music quickly. Daily sight-reading of new pieces is a skill that was emphasized in my early piano training and has served me well as a singer. It is a valuable tool for building tonal memory and confidence in one's ability to go forward when the music becomes more difficult to decipher. It promotes boldness and accuracy in learning new repertoire and takes away the fear of making a mistake, especially when rehearsing with other musicians for the first time. However, I have not found this to be a ritual that singers use on a regular basis. In my experience, it is beneficial for a singer, especially in the classical genre, to hone piano skills and become proficient at sight-reading to become an independent thinker when learning new repertoire, thus building a laudable reputation as a strong, reliable performer.

Practice! Practice! Practice! Every student in the performing arts has heard those words from a teacher, coach, or stage director. Still, too many young artists practice their art too little, practice incorrectly, or feel that it is irrelevant to the outcome and practice not at all, assuming they will be able to tap into some divine source of creativity when the performance date arrives. This false thinking and lack of preparation might actually work for a little while but will inevitably catch up with the performer, causing technical or musical mistakes and an accumulation of anxiety that can derail a performance.

To achieve a peak performance, one must feel in control, self-assured, and well prepared, with a mind that is calm and can concentrate easily on what is at hand. When preparation is lacking, an unsettling fear creeps into the psyche; worry and negativity overtake the senses; the body becomes tense; breathing lacks fluidity; and a smooth technique becomes a challenge. Relaxation and performance flow are no longer easy to achieve.

The development of a consistent, workable practice schedule is essential to technical and musical progress. The idea that one can achieve high-level performance skills while practicing five hours on Saturday and rarely singing or playing their instrument throughout the week is folly. This kind of practice schedule can be quite harmful to the voice. It can promote mental and physical fatigue in performers of all kinds; it does not gradually build technical skills, nor does it produce the stamina required for the demands of a performance career.

Some musicians are self-directed and don't need to write out details for daily practice, but most find it useful until the routine is completely established. Warm-up exercises, technical skill practice, and music to be rehearsed—with a specific goal for each piece—should be listed for every practice session. Armed with these objectives, it is less likely the musician will feel depressed or at sea in a practice room and waste precious time, not knowing what to do next as each goal is checked off the list. At the end of every practice session, there should be an assessment of things achieved. This promotes a feeling of accomplishment, mental lightness, and anticipation of future progress at having moved forward in technique or repertoire. So, a regular rehearsal schedule must be developed with specific goals in mind for each session to build confidence, technical ability, and endurance.

Here are a few tips for practice that I have found useful that will help to get you started.

1. Decide what to practice before going to the practice area—write out a plan.
2. Practice regularly—not in spurts.
3. Prepare the mind and body with positive self-talk and a few stretching or relaxation exercises before beginning the session.
4. Don't guess—learn the right notes.
5. Work on the difficult parts of a piece first.
6. Practice a variety of pieces in each session—don't obsess over just one, which can cause tension to build in the voice.
7. Overlearn everything—if you think you know it after ten repetitions, practice it at least ten more.
8. If you can't learn it by yourself, pay a coach to teach you.
9. Practice when you are rested and can concentrate.
10. Don't continue to sing if the voice is hoarse or the throat is sore.
11. Practice in a place where you are not distracted by noise, family obligations, or friends.
12. Take short breaks during a long practice session—repeat stretching exercises and positive self-talk during the breaks.
13. Keep well hydrated with plain water at room temperature—no soft drinks, milk, or sugary drinks to "goo" up the voice.
14. Be aware of good posture and proper technique at all times during the session.
15. Watch yourself in a mirror to practice desired facial expressions and catch bad physical habits, such as a jutting chin or muscle tension in the neck.
16. Evaluate the practice session when finished.
17. Put items that were not accomplished on the top of the list for the next session.
18. Congratulate yourself out loud for accomplishments.

It seems logical that one would attempt to find out all of the details about a performance engagement before signing on for the event. But that is not always the case. Sometimes inexperience or the mere excitement of being asked to perform clouds the gray cells, causing one to make incorrect assumptions about just what is expected as a performance outcome.

My professional performing career began during my doctoral studies at George Peabody College, where I learned that it is best to ask questions up front to save rehearsal time, rid the mind of worry, and reach appropriate performance goals. My voice teacher, having realized that I liked contemporary music, recommended me as the soloist for two pieces that would be featured on an international electronic music symposium headed up by Dr. Gilbert Trythall, a well-known composer and theorist. It was a massive festival that brought big crowds and lots of composers to the university to hear new, experimental music. This was the 1970s, when festivals like this were popular. They often involved audience participation and showcased pieces that required performers to do extravagant, bizarre things, such as crawling through long billowy tubes, turning radios on and off in the middle of works, and performing in other nontraditional ways within the concert space. They were precursors of the performance art genre and other nontraditional, extraordinary musical spectacles created since that time.

The two pieces I was given to sing were quite difficult. One was *Voices*, by Ramon Zupko, for voice and electronic tape; the other, *The Sears Box*, by Otto Henry, was to be sung a cappella. I don't have perfect pitch—rather, very good relative pitch. So, I worked like a demon to get all the difficult, angular intervals exactly right. The Otto piece, having no instrumental pitch references anywhere, was the most difficult since the word *melody* did not apply to any part of it. Knowing that the composer would be listening, I was a little concerned about two short sections of it, worried that I might miss a couple of intervals. When I walked onto the stage for the rehearsal, Dr. Trythall said, "OK, we have to ground you first." I had no idea what he meant. To my surprise, there was a little black box (the Sears Box, I presume) sitting on the edge of the stage to which a throat microphone was connected. He attached wires to my wrist and handed me the small, flat disk to place on the side of my throat. He explained that the sound of my voice would be picked up at the vocal cord level by the throat mic. Little did I know that the sound projecting to the audience would be a gargling noise with little pitch definition. I couldn't believe that I had spent hours trying to get all of those pitches exactly right and no one would be able to tell if they were right or not. Apparently, it was various levels of static that the composer was trying to achieve. There was no indication on the score that any of this would take place. I certainly knew my stuff in this case but could have saved a lot of worry if I had just asked if there was anything unusual about this piece that was not evident on the score. I learned that no question is too ridiculous to ask when accepting a performance engagement.

GET ORGANIZED

The performer who has a dream, is organized, knows what needs to be done, and has a plan to get there will be a step ahead of the rest. The presence of structure and order in a musician's life and personal habits helps to facilitate the establishment of a total performance package. It requires vision, determination, and outside advice if the organization of details concerning daily routine and career planning does not come naturally. Some singers appear to have been born with an "organization gene" that directs every aspect of their lives, moving them smoothly into the professional ranks, while others look like a train wreck about to happen due to a scattered approach to everything connected to making art and daily living. This haphazardness can negatively affect their ability to move from the student to the professional level as they attempt to develop a lasting career.

Some performers concentrate only on the outer wrapping when embarking on public performance and don't spend enough time with details that underpin a career, neglecting the nuts and bolts of the organization process. Much like a UPS package, the outside may look unblemished, but if the contents were not packed with care, they can come unglued, get broken, and result in disappointment for the recipient.

It doesn't matter if your to-do list is on your laptop or written neatly on a lined yellow pad. The manner in which you organize your life and daily routine is personal preference. Some singers happily carry around a little black book of names of contacts and a notebook with lists (I being one of those), while others can't move forward without a smart phone. Old-fashioned or modern matters not when it comes to getting things done. There seem to be two organizational problems encountered most often by performers: making a list but never following it or never bothering to make the list at all. In either case, chaos can thrive: a performer can become overwhelmed by details, make hurried decisions that may result in bad career choices, miss scheduled meetings or rehearsals, and develop chronic lateness due to a lack of organization.

Many aspects of a performer's existence are affected by an ability to organize effectively, including the establishment of a workable and enjoyable lifestyle, the adherence to professional commitments, networking, the development of a professional image in performances and interviews, and the presentation of a polished appearance on paper, on the phone, in person, through e-mail, and on social networking.

It is important to keep good, thorough records of all transactions, such as copies of contracts, e-mail that details schedule information—be sure to have a hard copy in case the Internet is down when you need it—and other correspondence that relates information about upcoming performances. There have been occasions when I received as many as twenty e-mails from concert organizers, some contradicting ones already sent. They contained information about host contacts, rehearsal and travel schedules, changes to established schedules, cuts or other changes to musical scores, program printing, costume fittings, attire for a concert and other related occasions, social events that I was expected to attend, and publicity interviews for which I had been scheduled. That's a lot of information to remember. I always put these items in a folder marked with the title of the event so that I will have everything in one place when I need it. Then, I take the folder with me to the engagement for reference during my downtime, to make sure I am at the right place at the right time and wearing the appropriate dress.

Another reason to keep good records is for tax purposes. Every performing artist needs to have a knowledgeable CPA with whom she or he can discuss needed documentation concerning tax exemptions that relate to one's performing life. If traveling for a concert, keep absolutely everything that relates to a trip: receipts for hotels, air flights, accompanist fees and their travel expenses that you cover, meals, taxis, the purchase of concert attire, and anything else that is allowed for deduction. Another kind of documentation that needs to be kept is a precise listing of any mileage for travel for rehearsals with other performers when you are driving your own vehicle. For example, if you live forty miles from your accompanist and have to travel to her location for rehearsals, then that mileage may be deductible since it is business related. This information should be recorded in a logbook, again with the dates clearly marked on a calendar. One should not become a hoarder, but these documents will need to be kept for several years in case you are audited. My CPA says that the IRS requires only three years but suggests keeping them five, to be safe. He also suggests keeping a copy of a calendar with the dates marked that coincide with receipts. It is never too early to begin that process, even if the singer is just beginning a career and has few items to list at that point on a tax return.

Reliability and punctuality are necessary organizational traits that must be ingrained in every serious performer. There is nothing more irritating for conductors, stage directors, or judges than waiting for a singer to show up for an audition or rehearsal. Performers have been excluded from auditions or fired from jobs for showing up late. Documented accidents can happen, causing a singer to arrive late to any event. In that case, you may be forgiven, but if it happens repeatedly, then the "always late" stigma will be placed after your name, and those in charge will think twice before engaging you as a performer. Singers must be diligent in keeping accurate records concerning all dates and times made for professional appointments, auditions, and rehearsals. To make those events go smoothly, always plan to arrive at the venue early, by at least thirty minutes. That will allow for transportation problems and give you time to freshen up before entering the performance arena.

The worst thing that a singer can do is simply not show up for a scheduled audition or rehearsal without informing anyone in advance. This leaves a very bad impression on the people in charge and may affect future auditions or employment. Illness or other emergencies can cause a singer to have to cancel, but notification must be given as soon as possible so that other arrangements can be made, replacements can be found, or events that involve you can be rescheduled. Your absence may still cause inconvenience, but you will have given those in authority the opportunity to reorganize and won't waste their valuable time waiting for you to arrive. You will be thought of as professional, thoughtful, and well organized.

Most performers, whether those just starting out or veterans, do not have personal assistants who arrange everything for them, pack their suitcases, and make sure that all details of an upcoming commitment are taken care of. Most performers are on their own. To feel calm, prepared, and ready to perform with as few snafus and distractions as possible, it is helpful to write down every element required to make a particular audition, performance, or rehearsal a success. Once that is done, items can be checked off during the assembly process, whether one is simply putting music into a briefcase for a concert across town or packing for an extended performance tour. This preparation makes the process go much faster and eliminates worry that something important has been left behind. There is nothing more heart-stopping than arriving at an audition to find that one of your needed pieces of music has been left at home on the piano or that you have brought the wrong top for the two-piece dress you plan to wear. But it happens frequently to the organizationally challenged.

I have observed singers come to auditions without having their music neatly organized for the staff accompanist, causing delays and much grumbling from the accompanist and the judges. I recall two occasions when singers have appeared for important auditions without appropriate attire, saying they forgot to pack it. These kinds of excuses rarely work unless the singer is such an extraordinary talent that nothing else matters—a rare event.

So, make a list and check it more than twice. The list should include every item you will need for the event:

- clothing to be worn;
- a copy of every piece of music to be used, clearly marked with any cuts you wish to take and, if copied, double-checked to make sure that none of the piano notes were cut off by the copier;
- documents required—airline and hotel confirmations, passports, and letters from agents and employers or those in charge of auditions; and

- a clearly typed, double-checked schedule of times for any events in which you are involved—rehearsals, concerts, warm-ups, interviews, travel schedule, and social events that surround them.

With all of this in hand, the performer can relax and concentrate on what is important—the music.

Finally, my best advice for those traveling to auditions or performances is this:

Find out everything you can about where you are going.

Always get there early.

Don't travel on the day of the event.

Don't pack your music or required medications in checked baggage, given that the airlines lost more than three thousand bags an hour in 2010.

Take only those things that you really need—don't be a packrat; you will find that you wear only about 20 percent of what you pack, and the rest will weigh you down. The lighter you can feel the better.

Staying connected to professional contacts is a must for every artist, and all avenues for communication should be employed. One of my faults is the seeming inability to remember anyone's name for more than five minutes after having been introduced to them. This has nothing to do with age. I've been this way all of my life. I've tried every kind of trick to remember names, and nothing works. So, I try to write down names of people I meet as soon as possible, or I get a business card from them with contact information so that I won't forget who they are when I need to get in touch.

Singers encounter hundreds of people as they go through academic preparation, the audition process, and public performances involved in building a career. It requires organization, effort, persistence, and a commitment to maintain a good relationship with as many people as possible, keeping contact with those for whom you have worked, auditioned, met casually, or befriended. Staying in touch is easy in today's world of Internet availability, but it has also become somewhat impersonal. The number of e-mails, tweets, and Facebook notices received in a day can be overwhelming, each one looking much like the other. The misspellings, half-sentences, lack of punctuation marks, no greeting or organization to the material, odd pictures, and personal confessions have become the norm and can give a bad impression of the sender, causing the receiver (some professional you want to impress) to simply press the delete button before getting to the end. As Betty White famously said about Facebook, "it seems like a huge waste of time."

One of the primary considerations for performers when getting organized is deciding how, when, and how often to make contact with others in the profession. More and more, people are feeling the need for the old-fashioned kind of personal contact that a handwritten thank-you note or a nicely typed letter provides. Since my college days, I've kept a list with the contact information of people met along the way in my career: fellow performers, composers, conductors, stage directors, and their friends. I made a point to contact them periodically by sending Christmas cards with a small updated bit of information about my career, a flier about (or a copy of) my book or CDs, a note about an upcoming professional engagement, a copy of a notable review in a major venue, or a formal letter with an updated vita.

These personal communications have been most useful and resulted in many of the professional engagements and recording opportunities I've had over the years. They reminded people who rarely saw me that I was still on the horizon and available when the right venue became apparent for my talents. These notes also kept up or created lasting friendships with people in the music profession. I discovered early on that you never know when you will meet that one person who will offer you a future performance opportunity. The contact may not be in a position to do so when you first meet, but situations change, and at some point your continued efforts to stay in touch may pay off in a big way.

While websites and social networks such as LinkedIn are useful and perhaps necessary for the budding artist, it never hurts to go the extra mile and present a more personal approach to the acquisition and maintenance of a positive relationship with possible future employers. Though there seems to be a danger that the U.S. Postal Service may go under, I still keep in contact with people through handwritten notes. Apparently, others are going back to this kind of communication. Much is being written about the lack of personal communication today and the delight with which people receive real mail, not e-mail. I recently read an article about the upsurge in creating handmade greeting cards. It isn't necessary to go that far, but a well-turned phrase written to convey a personal thank-you to someone who took the time to hear your audition, talk with you about a possible future engagement, or provide needed information may keep you in that person's mind much longer than the quickly ripped-off e-mail that looks sloppy and forgets a greeting.

SPEAK UP

One of my tenor friends told me that he would rather sing a thousand songs than say two words to an audience. He is like many singers who have an overwhelming fear of speaking in a formal situation, though singing gives them no pause. Their normal, well-projected singing tone turns into a breathy, squeaky, hard-to-understand mumble when required to speak from the stage or answer questions from audition judges.

It is also quite disconcerting for viewers to watch singers fidget, stare at the floor, whisper, read mechanically, or ramble through a bit of vital information. Anything spoken during a performance, audition, or interview should be considered part of the performance, not an adjunct to it, and prepared as carefully as the music to be sung or played.

Not all performers respond in such a negative way to the use of their own speaking voices. Many find it quite natural to move from one form of vocalization to another without feeling that some personality switch has been flipped when asked to speak. I definitely fall into that category. I feel much less nervous if I can use my speaking voice in a normal manner from the stage, then move on to singing. I like to use that tactic to bring the audience over to my side from the beginning and feel that I've known them forever. This is especially helpful in a recital situation. So, I try to find something welcoming to say or give a short bit of information early in a recital or chamber concert (if appropriate) about a composer or a song text. It breaks the ice for the audience and me. I have found that listeners respond well to short, well-projected introductions or a bit of humor. Some audience members have made a point to thank me after concerts, especially those in which I was singing experimental music, and expressed their appreciation that I brought them more personally into the performance by talking to them as if they were friends, not adversaries.

I encourage my voice students to start speaking in public at an early age, announcing their pieces in master classes and local concerts, so that by the time they are ready to use their speaking voice in a professional situation, it feels quite natural to do so. Some take to this immediately, while others balk and require more persuasion to give it a try. In either case, I often suggest that they take a speech class or become involved in a theatrical play, which will give them additional tools and experiences to achieve their goals.

One might think that this apprehension about speaking applies only to those who are painfully shy, but it seems to favor no particular personality type. My aforementioned tenor friend certainly is not shy; he speaks with a clear, well-placed tone in casual situations and has no problem expressing original ideas. However, he and others like him lack confidence in their speaking voice and find that it seems to disappear when they have to talk to people in auditions and performances, even if the spoken material has been prepared in advance.

Performers often experience even more difficulty appearing comfortable and spontaneous when speaking off the cuff in front of an audience or in publicity interviews on radio and television that might occur before a performance. Those who accept invitations to do radio and television interviews are especially at risk if they are ill-prepared for that kind of venue; it is not natural to their personality, and they simply try to wing it without giving any thought to the content that might be discussed. I have enjoyed participating in several interviews on public radio and television over the years, from Nashville's WPLN-FM to Boston's WCRB-FM. Sometimes, they were publicity interviews for the release of current recordings or upcoming concerts in those cities, while on three occasions, they consisted of interviews and live performances combined, including one for WDCN public television in Nashville and *Chamber Works* on WGBH-FM in Boston.

In each case, I knew the general parameters of the discussion that would take place, made sure that I could talk about the music that had been recorded or was to be performed in concert, and thought about answers I would give to other topics that the interviewer might ask about, including my musical training and performance background, how I worked with other musicians, how I chose the music to be recorded or performed, my relationship with some of the living composers on the program of works, and what my future performance goals were. In all cases, those questions were actually asked, plus others that related to issues that were brought up in the discussion as a result of my answers. My personality seems to fit that kind of scenario, so I never felt ill at ease; I enjoyed the chats with some intriguing radio and television hosts. But if a performer's personality does not suit this kind of venue or one is not willing to work on an ability to cope with them by utilizing interview practice sessions with coaches or persons in the communications arts, it may be best to avoid them. Sometimes, an inability to speak with spontaneity, confidence, clarity, and an appropriate vocabulary, coupled with the lack of preparation given to what will be said, can cause a performer to blurt out things that should not be said at all, causing embarrassment for all concerned. So, the preparation and rehearsal of anything to be spoken in front of people as part of an audition, performance, or interview is as important as the rehearsal of material to be sung.

I have judged numerous performers in vocal competitions whose singing voices were resonant and could carry well in a large concert hall over an orchestra but were almost inaudible when they introduced themselves and their repertoire to a panel of judges in a medium-sized room. It seems to be a common problem and one that needs to be addressed before embarking on professional auditions, interviews, or talking from a concert stage.

In an audition, singers may be required to answer questions or announce repertoire. In a performance situation, they may choose to enlighten the audience with information about the content of the program. In either case, an ineffective delivery of the speaking voice can sabotage an otherwise excellent performance, causing the singer to appear self-conscious and lack sufficient confidence to win over those listening. So, every performer must address these issues of voice projection, preparation of speaking material, and appropriateness of the content so that a total package of confidence is presented, whether singing or speaking.

Singers who shrink at the thought of speaking from the stage can gain confidence in several ways. Practical solutions exist for those singers who normally speak very softly or have trouble speaking without fry tones or gravel in the voice. They may need to work with a professional speech therapist to modulate the range and dynamics possibilities of the speaking voice. The correction of any speaking faults will be a healthy tool for singing as well as speaking. So, this work should be done as much to save the singing voice any stress as to create a usable speaking voice for the stage.

Once a clearly projected normal range has been achieved for the speaking voice, it is essential to practice speaking from the stage using that range and tone, not one that is feigned for a special occasion. I recently attended a recital in which the singer chose to tell the audience about two pieces that might be unfamiliar to them. Having heard the singer's natural speaking voice many times in casual situations, I was caught off guard when she began to speak to the audience in a vocal range that was a good bit higher than normal, looping the vocal inflexion up and down (almost like *sprechstimme*) and with a hint of a British accent. I'm certain that she had never been to England. The man sitting next to me, who knew her, whispered in my ear, "Where did that accent come from?" The effect was quite comical, not what she had hoped, I'm sure. It is helpful to practice speaking in a projected voice for someone who knows you well to get much-needed feedback, perhaps recording your voice and listening to it to make sure that it sounds natural.

The next thing to consider is whether to speak at all. Classical singers performing in operas or orchestral or chamber music concerts are rarely asked or given the opportunity to speak to the audience. However, solo recitalists, those who sing contemporary classical music (whether with one instrument or an ensemble), and opera singers presenting scenes or workshops for students often speak to the audience about pieces included on the program. In that case, anything that a singer decides to say to the audience must be planned with brevity, content, and emotional tone in mind. There is nothing more painful than listening to a performer drone on too long in a monotone speaking voice, boring the audience with disorganized information about a musical selection that may be shorter in length than the explanation given. The attention of the audience will be lost before the first note is sung, something that may be difficult to recapture.

Some concert halls have less-than-desirable acoustics for singing or speaking, while others may project the singing voice adequately but only in the upper register or at a very high volume level. It can be a difficult task to speak in a normal range with good projection, being heard clearly in the back of a hall like this, such a dead space. In this case, the singer must decide whether to attempt to speak at all and, if so, whether to use a microphone when speaking to the audience, if the singing will be performed without one. The obvious difference in sound quality and volume level, when switching back and forth, can be disconcerting and cause the singing voice to sound distant and lack vibrancy, after the audience has become used to the presence of sound afforded them with the microphone. It is a psychological problem as well as an auditory one for the listener, and it is one that the singer should consider before choosing to do it. However, if the use of a microphone seems appropriate, then familiarity with microphone technique must be addressed. Too often, singers and speakers approach a microphone as if it is an implement brought back from some NASA mission—looking at it as if they don't know whether or how to turn it on or how far to hold it in front of the mouth, letting it loll back and forth in front of the face, never quite hitting the right mark for clear speech—none of which projects the voice well nor presents the singer in a professional manner. So, if microphone technique is foreign to the singer, she or he needs to work with a technician and learn how to use one correctly so that it sounds and looks natural. Since not all microphones are created equal and each performance space is different in sound quality, there must be a sound check before any event in which a microphone is used so that the performer knows that it is working, how much presence it has, and how close to the mouth it must be held to get the proper sound desired. Once this is done, the performer can feel more confident in using it when needed, and the audience will not be frustrated by a lack of consistent sound projection or notice any lack of attention to preparation for its use.

Finally, the physical manner in which a person speaks is mightily important. We all have physical habits that become magnified when we stand alone on the stage. Some people gesture wildly with their hands or constantly twirl the ring on the fourth finger of their left hand; others pace back and forth; and many talk to the ceiling or the floor while ignoring the audience in the middle. Any of these negative physical attributes can cause those watching to focus on the wrong thing and miss the point of what you are trying to say.

Once your voice has been properly elevated and its spoken content honed, practice in front of a mirror to get a good mind's-eye picture of your facial expressions, body language, and any annoying physical habits that you need to curtail. Then, get the opinion of someone you trust who will tell you the truth about any distractions that linger in the presentation. It will make a huge difference in your confidence level when you get onstage, knowing that you have worked out most of the kinks in your delivery.

All of these considerations apply to auditions and interviews as well. In such competitive situations, body language, facial expressions, eye contact, and the content of your speech will be scrutinized from the moment you enter the room until you leave. Every aspect of your appearance and personality will raise or lower your prospects in the eyes of the judges. So, care must be given to present your best self with intelligible, intelligent speech that has a filter when needed. This is not the time to blabber on about your personal life or subjects that are unrelated to the purpose at hand. Several books are listed at the back of this volume to help with audition preparation. They contain valuable information that serious artists should be aware of so that auditions and interviews will go more smoothly and there will be fewer surprises and disappointments caused by poor speaking habits or unsuitable body language.

* * *

REMINDERS!

- Develop professional behavior.
- Prepare thoroughly and pay attention to details.
- Never make excuses to judges, an audience, or employers.
- Establish an effective practice routine.
- Upgrade your piano skills and sight-reading ability.
- Ask necessary questions before accepting engagements.
- Make organization of details a priority.
- Keep good records.
- Make a list of items required for auditions or performances.
- Stay connected to professional contacts.
- Learn to speak in public as easily and spontaneously as you sing.

SIX

It Takes a Village

No one should attempt to achieve a successful career in performance alone. All artists need advocates in their lives to succeed, reach lofty goals, and feel free to express artistic ideas—whether mainstream or on the edge. Without a safety net filled with supporters, performing artists—especially young ones—may find it difficult to stay aloft when there are so many career pressures, distractions, financial considerations, and family issues to deal with on a daily basis.

As I look back over my career, it is obvious to me that some of it would have been rudimentary, boring, ordinary, physically draining, and nothing much to write about if not for the people I met along the way. There were many talented, inspirational, generous, funny—even quirky—individuals who brought stimulating artistic ideas to rehearsals and performances of musical repertoire, contributed much-needed humor to frustrating or complicated situations, cordially hosted me for concert or operatic performances, and supported my musical whims, no matter how bizarre or experimental. Many have become lifelong friends because of an association that began due to a concert engagement. In a very real sense, that friendship may be the most important result of the intent of our original meeting, much more valuable than the performance itself.

BE COLLABORATIVE

Solo a cappella music is lovely, but it is the rare singer who always wants to sing alone, never to interact with other musicians. Realistically, it is practically impossible to build a career in performance without collaboration and artistic connection to others. Therefore, performers must make it a priority to be verbally appreciative, artistically responsive, and flexible when dealing with those who clear their paths and facilitate details—whether musical or organizational—on the way to the end of every performance. Though every performer should strive to develop definitive artistic ideas concerning musical expression and be prepared to verbalize those ideas with conviction to those with whom they will make music, the contributions and expertise of collaborators should be respected and never abused. Some personality types find it hard collaborating with anyone, always feel the need to be in charge, like to bark orders, and shun any ideas other than their own. Their harsh treatment or intellectual and creative dismissal of those with whom they work can be distressing, result in atmospheric tension and a poor performance outcome, and may mark them as a poison to avoid for future engagements.

Musical partners (accompanists and chamber players) and performing organizations (orchestras, opera and musical theatre companies, and choral ensembles) have limits as to the amount of verbal or situational strife they are willing to endure during the rehearsal and performance process. Some limits may be stated in a contract or letter, but most are unwritten, only emotionally or structurally felt. When some unharmonious line is crossed by a performer's strident attitude, discord becomes overwhelming, and musical goals are difficult to achieve for all involved. At that point, the performer's contribution may find few supporters. The niggly performer with an overbearing personality will have to have superhuman talent to make collaborators want to work with him or her on a continuing basis. So, unless a prickly performer sees how his or her actions are received, becomes more flexible, and understands how to work better with collaborators, a career can be derailed for lack of cooperative understanding, since those who must work with him or her need a very good reason to do so.

Most singers spend a great part of their performing lives working with pianists, either as rehearsal accompanists for opera, musical theatre, and orchestral performances or to prepare jazz and pop concerts and classical recital repertoire that just involves the two of them. In the latter case, magical things happen if a special bond develops as the two work out musical ideas, read each other's musical minds, and play off interpretative shadings brought out by the other. When this kind of relationship matures, extraordinarily phantasmagorical and wonderful things can occur—things that are unspoken and unplanned, things that both performers marvel at after the performance, things that listeners comment on with awe. It is a wondrous experience for the singer when her or his every nuance, color change, and stylistic interpretation is matched perfectly and seamlessly at the piano, no matter the musical style being performed. To make that kind of beautiful music together, a singer needs a pianist who can read her or his mind, has similar ideas about musical expression, and will tolerate all kinds of eccentricities that singers seem to possess.

Sometimes, singers have to work with several pianists before finding just the right musical and intellectual fit for their particular artistic expression. It can be an exhausting process over a period of time before the right connection is made. Unfortunately, some never find it. But those who are lucky know it when it happens. The singer is suddenly aware that the music can simply flow from the voice, body, and mind without any barriers being created by some extraneous force pulling in an opposite direction from the piano.

That kind of musical EQ relationship does not come along every day. There have been many famous classical singer/pianist partners who seemed to perform as one entity; memorable examples include baritone Dietrich Fischer-Dieskau and pianist Gerald Moore, as well as mezzo-soprano Jan De Gaetani and pianist Gilbert Kalish. When those duos were onstage together, magic definitely happened. As with all of life's relationships, the ideal singer and pianist duo is a hard one to find and maintain. When it does happen, the cultivation process must be attentive, continuing, and always collaborative.

I was one of the lucky ones. I have had the opportunity to sing with several fine pianists over the years, but I was extremely fortunate to work with two extraordinary musical partners who enhanced every joint effort and made my performing life a great pleasure: Rosemary Platt, one of my collaborative pianists in the late 1980s and early 1990s for several premieres and recitals and two recordings, and Patsy Wade, whom I met in graduate school and who has been my most constant musical partner for thirty-five years, joining me for dozens of concerts in the United States and Europe, five recordings, and premieres of more than thirty works by American and British composers. In both cases, when I had the good fortune to perform with them, my mind was free to concentrate only on musical expression because I knew that if I decided to go off a cliff, they would gladly follow or race me to the edge, having had the thought first. That kind of simpatico is priceless and should never be taken lightly. It must be cultivated due to its rarity.

Too often, singers, especially students, take excellent, attentive accompanists' time for granted, do not think of them as equal partners in music making, nor give them the artistic respect they deserve. I have heard accompanists complain that singers miss scheduled rehearsals without bothering to cancel or explain, wait until the last minute to give them a stack of difficult music to play at the next day's rehearsal, and become miffed if the accompanist doesn't play every note perfectly within twenty-four hours. This kind of mistreatment can cause an accompanist to be a bit put off (to say the least) by the singer's lateness, self-centeredness, and lack of professionalism. It probably means that the singer has presented such a bad impression that the accompanist may never play for him or her again and will likely spread the word to other pianists who might be asked. A negative reputation can cause a singer to have difficulty in finding a good accompanist when one is badly needed. Apparently, those singers are thinking of themselves only as soloists—not as collaborators—and have not yet learned that good accompanists are busy people, that it takes time to prepare piano accompaniments well, and that the pianist can make or break a singer's performance.

Most singers forget the words to a song or aria now and then, and I have certainly had my share. The mind can play tricks and seem to go blank on the most familiar pieces. It happens all the time, as some famous singers have notoriously experienced when singing "The Star-Spangled Banner" on television. The backlash can be terrible in a situation like that, where everyone knows the words to such an important traditional piece. To be safe, it's best to have them written out on a small piece of paper to carry with you in case of a memory block. But most of the time, even if the audience knows the words, it won't be judgmental as long as you sing something that seems to fit the music. Singers have to learn to make the words up and go on without any indication of distress, as if it had been written that way. If you stop in the middle of the piece and go around to the piano to look at the music or wait for the pianist to give you the words, the audience gets nervous and the mood is ruined. When unexpected things like this happen, a singer will be forever grateful to a savvy, sympathetic accompanist who saves the day. So the cultivation of a relationship of trust and respect must take top priority for those singers who need a collaborative pianist.

I could write another book about the number of times my pianists have saved me during a performance, but I will relive only one graphic experience here, a memorable event that Patsy Wade and I still laugh about. I was asked to sing a recital at the University of Tennessee, Knoxville, several years ago for a regional convention of voice teachers and their students. The program was a showcase for American music and included a short song cycle (*Three Love Songs*) by Julia Smith. I expected that a few of the teachers in the audience would know this music but that it would be new to most of them. I had sung the cycle several times before, including a performance at Merkin Concert Hall in New York City with Smith in the audience. So, being prepared and remembering the words was not an issue. The first two songs went beautifully, no problems. As Patsy played the introduction to the final song, I remember thinking, "What is that piece? It doesn't even sound familiar." She repeated the introduction while I waited for some kind of recognition to creep into my brain. None did. She kept playing, improvising around the opening themes. Finally, I decided that I really needed to sing something. So, for the next few minutes, we both had an out-of-body experience. I made up words about love and things that related to it while Patsy somehow knew where I was going harmonically and melodically. She followed me, then led me, playing in between my phrases, creating motives and whole sections of music in the style of Julia Smith.

At some point, we collectively decided that it was time to end the song. I took my bow, gestured to her to take a bow, and we exited the stage completely amazed at what had just happened. No one seemed to notice that I had no idea what I was doing. Apparently, our foray into composition was convincing because one of the voice teachers who talked with me after the concert asked where I found that version of the third song. She said she liked it better than the original and wanted to know if I had found an unpublished version through my research into music by women composers. Fortunately, I never had to answer the question because the organizer of the event swept us away for pictures. Having spent some time with Julia Smith in New York, I believe that she would have chuckled at this and enjoyed our little escapade. I have no idea what it really sounded like since that concert was not recorded—Patsy says that my words actually rhymed—but it still amazes me when I think about the synchrony with which Patsy maneuvered through such a minefield without a glitch instead of throwing up her hands and letting me die a slow death.

When searching for the perfect collaborative pianist or other musical partner in any artistic endeavor, it is important to take notice of the person's personality, temperament, level of musicianship, and lifestyle characteristics as you rehearse and discuss musical ideas. The ease with which this musical preparation process flows can help you decide whether this person is a perfect fit for your own talents and temperament. If there seems to be a lot of discord in the rehearsal, leading to a negative outcome, then the singer must move on and find another partner. There is nothing worse than leaving a rehearsal and feeling irritated due to personality conflicts or feeling frustrated that it was a great waste of time, musically.

Over many years of working with pianists and other musicians for my own performances and for singers I've coached, I have encountered several negative attributes to look out for when dealing with musical partners. There was the pianist who continued to smoke through rehearsals and whose clothes reeked of it—something no singer should endure—and the string player who was so scattered that he forgot where the rehearsal was to take place and showed up several miles away, causing a two-hour delay. Then there was the flighty pianist who realized that he had left his music at home and hurriedly photocopied the singer's copy ten minutes before the performance, did not put it in a notebook, forgot to get a page turner, and kept picking up the pages from the piano bench as the songs progressed, since the piano rack was not large enough to string out all of the pages across it—very distracting for the audience. Finally, there was the pianist who had the music months in advance, played it differently in tempo and accuracy at each rehearsal, and subsequently started two songs in the wrong key on the performance, requiring the singer to have to stop while the pianist began again in the correct key. All of these are red flags and good reasons to move on to other collaborative partners to get the best possible result from your performance. Assuming that the singer is professional, prepared, and considerate, the partner must also be reciprocative for the duo experience to be productive and enjoyable.

Several professional and personal characteristics stand out as ones that can make or break such an important relationship.

The partner must possess a flexible temperament that works well with others. Pianists can be very helpful in making musical decisions and correcting any errors that might have been learned by a singer, but no singer needs a pianist who comes to rehearsals with nothing but criticism about the music to be performed, the singer's voice and musicianship, or the amount of time that has to be spent in rehearsal for an upcoming event. Singers have plenty of their own self-generated negativity to deal with, so they don't need some outside source constantly reminding them of some vocal fault or lack of musical ability, especially when nearing a performance date.

Lifestyle similarities are important considerations when choosing musical partners. Incompatible personal habits can disrupt rehearsals, cause friction or delays, and become especially annoying if it is necessary to travel together for concert engagements. Issues such as the use of substances (alcohol, tobacco, and mood-altering drugs), incessant talking, bodily hygiene, and a similar sleep-work schedule may determine whether the person matches your lifestyle. Performers often ignore these personal characteristics until they find themselves cooped up in a hotel room for days with someone whose habits make life miserable, in which case separate hotel rooms are a must.

The pianist should be able to play at a performance level equal to that of the singer and come to rehearsals prepared to play with accuracy and confidence. It is a great waste of time and quite depressing for a singer to have a pianist who practices the music only when rehearsing with you, has given no thought to musical interpretation, and is still playing many wrong notes rehearsal after rehearsal.

A pianist needs to keep commitments to scheduled rehearsals and performance dates. Musicians who seem unorganized, forget scheduled dates, always show up late, or cancel at the last minute can drive you crazy and waste your time, no matter how well they play their instrument.

Musical sensitivity to the collaborative effort is crucial. After all, you are the one who has to sing those long phrases in one breath or linger just the right amount of time on a particular word. If the pianist isn't listening to you but is instead focused on only the piano part, doesn't pay attention to how you want to phrase, plays on without realizing you are still holding that high note, or doesn't have the musical sensitivity to understand why you are phrasing in a certain way, the outcome will be disastrous. Collaboration of this sort is no collaboration at all, in which case another musical partner must be found—quickly.

To expand and sustain a performance career, musicians need to become curious and inventive and seek out creative partners of many kinds. Some singers are satisfied to limit collaborations to only one or two people, staying locked in to the same performance format and locale forever. However, many singers find this kind of artistic existence confining and move toward audience expansion, musical experimentation, and the flowering of their imagination as performance goals. Decisions made concerning collaboration can affect a singer's career exponentially, both geographically and creatively. For some performers, originality in thinking and the development of performance concepts can certainly thrive in isolation. However, at some point, even a self-motivated genius who desires an audience must find ways to get ideas out into the world to grow a reputation as a professional musician who has much to offer in public performance. Collaboration with other musical artists is one of the best ways to achieve that goal.

For many performers who are not self-starters and need inspiration to enliven and channel creative thinking, isolation can be deadly. It can stall a career in performance, stunt inventiveness, and cause performances to be uninteresting due to a lack of ideas flooding in from outside sources. So, no matter the intellectual curiosity and nature of the musician, performers cannot afford isolation, just sitting in the shadows and waiting for others to come looking for their talent. Instead, they must find ways to connect with as many people in their performance genre as possible to plant seeds for future performance opportunities, to gain employment, and to spark creative thinking.

In today's world, versatility, inquisitiveness, and experimentation are key factors in career development. To accomplish this, it is useful and creatively stimulating to establish a dialogue with other kinds of creative artists who have complementary talents, whether they are of a similar performance bent or have like background and training. When connections are made with creative people outside one's familiar circle, exciting and forward-thinking projects can develop that invigorate performers, cause them to see their art in a new way, and promote enthusiasm about the future of their careers.

A burgeoning area of collaboration is cross-pollination of genres. It is taking place all over the music industry at present and becoming the norm rather than the exception. Classical performers are playing and singing with musicians from the bluegrass, jazz, or pop music world; jazz and country artists are performing with symphony orchestras; classic pop stars are making albums with rockers and rappers; and classical singers are incorporating dance, art exhibits, poetic readings, and photography into the traditional recital format. There is no limit to the possibilities of productive collaboration, except that of the individual artist's lack of imagination or desire to take a chance and branch out in the profession. So, to isolate oneself from possible colleagues or to limit one's artistic talent to only one small bit of the universe of creativity can be career stifling, cause a performing artist to feel depressed for lack of public attention, and provide no stimulus for inventive thinking.

These kinds of collaborations could also be undertaken with artists from genres outside a singer's art form. This is especially true for those performers who also work in a university, arts academy, or conservatory setting where poets and writers, painters, dancers, conductors, directors, photographers, arrangers, composers, and actors may be available as sources for artistic interaction and collaboration. Singers regularly encounter many of these kinds of artists while performing in concert venues, opera or musical theatre productions, and professional interview situations. Each may have some aspect of their art that will spark an intriguing idea for investigation.

Early in my career, I took a teaching job at what was then a small university in a small city not known for classical music offerings. Though both the university and the city have grown substantially since that time, I realized back then that to build a performance career, I would need to actively develop an audience for my talent, create my own performance opportunities, and make professional contacts with artists outside my geographical area and performance specialization. Many singers share that scenario. There may be no existing concert series in which their singing style and repertoire fit and no clamoring group of fans awaiting their latest recital program.

Though I sang traditional recital and chamber music repertoire both on campus and in other venues around the region, I was particularly interested in performing and promoting contemporary classical music, something that had not been done previously at my university. So, I took this void as an opportunity to start a contemporary music series called Dimensions, which began its run in 1981. Though it started as a local, on-campus collaboration with one or two other music faculty members, it became a much larger entity that thrived for twenty-eight years. During its tenure, sixty composers of national and international reputation came to the campus for performances and lectures to students; fifty-six premieres were given; and more than forty guest artists performed in the series.

The series started small, with one performance the first year, but it eventually grew to three or four on-campus concerts each year, student performer concerts, a grant-funded CD, and a touring program that drew an enthusiastic audience of students, faculty, and local residents. It was also cited as one of the keystone elements in the state-funded Center of Excellence for the Performing Arts, which the university received in 1985, one of the current Centers of Excellence still in existence in Tennessee. I could not have done this by myself. Though it started as a way for me and one other member of the music faculty to present new music, the series would not have been successful without the creative input and vital energy brought to this venture by many other people. To achieve the stated goals for the series, it took collaboration with like-minded colleagues in the music department and other kinds of artist faculty across campus from the departments of art, theatre, foreign language, and creative writing to bring much of this new repertoire to life for an eager audience that began to expect to see and hear something unique at each performance.

An initial desire to develop a contemporary music venue for my own performance interests culminated in an enormous opportunity for me and others on campus to connect with creative people from a much larger geographical area and artistic spectrum. It put me in contact with dozens of people that I would never have met otherwise, many of whom subsequently gave me opportunities for performances in other venues. So, when you find yourself in a physical place that does not offer performance possibilities for your talent, don't wait to be discovered. Get busy and make things happen! Even the smallest steps in the direction you wish to go can bring big dividends when you increase your network of contacts for collaboration.

In the performance world, individual links in a chain of collaborative contacts can lead to an interesting and self-propelling career full of new ideas, intriguing people, and adventures that may not have been imagined. For example, I have no talent for composition but have always been fascinated by the process. Having realized early in my career that my specific area of performance expertise seemed to be in contemporary classical music, I decided to seek out composers who were writing music for my voice type. After a good bit of research, I found a few regional composers who were writing music that I simply adored. I contacted them and discovered that they were very glad to hear from me. Most stated that they had difficulty finding professional solo singers who were interested in singing new music, though their instrumental or choral music was getting a good bit of attention. I had found a wonderful collaborative outlet. Suddenly, I was singing premieres, having composers write music for me, recording new works, and meeting fascinating people who had access to performance venues that I would never have known about or been engaged for if not for those contacts with composers.

The links in the chain grew. As other composers on the regional, national, and international levels found out that I was available, interested, and capable of singing new works, whether composed in a more traditional style or as experimental works with extravagant vocal techniques, more performance opportunities and engagements came my way. Some composers heard me sing at new music festivals or conferences on music by women composers and made a point to see me after my performance to leave contact information and scores of their works—and I found some real gems among them—or to inquire about my availability to sing on some future event. In each case, I always made a point to follow up on every inquiry, invitation, or suggestion for performance repertoire. This was a great learning period for me. By reading through so much new music, working with living composers, and listening to their perspective about the music's intent, I found my musical voice and became more confident that I was better able to determine what I really wanted to spend my time singing.

Because of my interest in composers and new music, I came into contact with performers from around the country whom I met at new music festivals. Several of these chance meetings culminated in new, unique collaborations that brought additional concert appearances, more premieres, and recording opportunities that I would not have had otherwise. This is the manner in which I met Rosemary Platt, the wonderful Ohio State University–based pianist with whom I made two recordings. She was in the audience when I sang a recital of music by women composers at the University of Michigan in 1983. After the concert, she came backstage, introduced herself, and said, "I have a recording series of music by women composers. So far, it has only included works for solo piano, but I want you to make the next one with me." Knowing of her extraordinary work and musicianship, I was stunned and flattered and said, "Yes, of course." That was the beginning of an incredible musical collaboration and continuing friendship that would not have happened if I had not pursued my interest in and collaboration with contemporary composers, both male and female.

Another link developed that brought even more collaborations. Due to performances of contemporary music for National Association of Teachers of Singing conventions and other venues, my research into contemporary music came to the attention of Richard Miller, the internationally known vocal pedagogue who was at that time the editor of the association's *Journal of Singing*. In 1985, he engaged me to write a quarterly column called "New Directions," which ran in every issue of the journal until 2009. As a result of those articles, I met and made friends with dozens of composers over the years, some of whom engaged me for performances and recordings of their works in the United States and England. So, one thing can easily lead to another and create strong links in a chain of events that will support a developing performance career if an artist keeps the door open to all kinds of creative collaborations.

DEVELOP A SUPPORT SYSTEM

The *New Oxford American Dictionary* gives many definitions for the word *support*. But the one that most applies to the kind of support needed by performing artists includes that which is manifested by "acts and attitudes that sustain a person, keeps their spirits high under trial or affliction, upholds and advocates for them under all circumstances, gives comfort and emotional help, encourages, and in some cases, provides for their maintenance, financially." That level of support will probably not come from one person alone. Rather, it will take several entities to cover all of those bases.

The performing life can be a lonely and frightening existence for those artists who do not have a reliable support system. Many discover quickly that the superficiality and fickleness of adoring fans is no good substitute. Other, more constant sources need to be found to bolster confidence or provide emotional strength and professional advice when necessary.

To have a well-defined, genuine, and solid support system of colleagues, friends, family, teachers or coaches, counselors, doctors, and other professionals in your field is a blessing and a necessity for any singer who is thrown into that world of seeming chaos that we call *performance*. Without it, a young artist can feel scattered and lonely, be easily manipulated into poor musical and lifestyle decisions, experience heightened performance anxiety for lack of a loyal and knowledgeable confidant, and find it difficult to enjoy the achievement of artistic goals and performance successes. Even veteran performers have been known to flounder when their long-time support system has broken down. So, performing artists must learn to identify, acknowledge, cultivate, and be thankful for any person or entity that bolsters their performance efforts by giving some kind of needed support.

Each singer must determine just how much and what kind of support he or she needs to lead a healthy, happy life as a performing artist. Some singers need an army of people to get them through circumstances that others seem to manage without much outside support. Support comes in many forms, has disparate functions, and is not always needed on a continuing basis. However, the sources for that support must be available to the singer when a condition demands it. Otherwise, a singer can feel as if there is no one to turn to for help in sticky situations and there is no one who cares if things go wrong or confidence flags.

Singers live in the same world as everybody else, but they are significantly different from the population at large in the way they think about the voice. Since the voice is their primary link to artistic expression and livelihood, they are more acutely aware that they have only one voice, which must be guarded from negative forces since it cannot be replaced with a new model. When it comes to the protection and use of the voice, singers tend to be a needy lot. Given that their instrument is invisible and controlled by forces both physical and psychological, it is no wonder that they often struggle not to obsess over subtle changes in vocal production and need reassurance concerning vocal health and technique. Being a singer myself, having taught dozens of singers and performed with many professional singers for forty years, I can state without reservation that some tend to require a lot of emotional and psychological support to keep the voice in peak performance condition. Also, since the voice reflects our emotional state when we speak or sing, it provides a window into whatever is going on in our lives and will be mirrored in its tone, strength, stamina, and steadiness. The voice can almost disappear if emotional strain becomes too much for the psyche to handle, not the kind of situation in which a singer should find oneself. That predicament can bring the demise of a particular performance or affect long-term goals if not addressed.

I've watched this kind of emotional roller coaster happen in voice lessons with students. I recall a recent coaching session that had been arranged with an advanced singer who was preparing for auditions. Normally, she was composed, skilled, confident, and quite upbeat, always entering my office with some cheery greeting. On this particular day, she entered quietly, did not make eye contact, plopped her books down on a chair, and seemed distracted when I asked how things were going for her. She said, "OK," but I knew something was wrong. She was not herself. As we started to work on her first aria, it was obvious that her voice sounded strained, thinner, and she began to fidget. I sensed that no matter how hard we tried, either she was ill, or her voice was being held back by something that had nothing to do with the music she was singing. So, I looked at her and asked, "Would you prefer to do this on another day?" As the last word came out of my mouth, she teared up and let out the sob that had been bottled up but already forecast by the alien singing voice she had just been using. Indeed, I found out that in this case, there was something terribly wrong. This kind of vocal reaction to inner strife is common for singers and can appear at the slightest upset. It doesn't have to involve some dire circumstance. After all, the voice is a reflection of the condition of the singer as a whole, and if the condition is not a happy one, then the voice is not happy.

Obviously, many events can occur in a performer's daily life that might cause the voice to reflect distress. It is unrealistic to believe that one can go through life without having an occasional upset of some kind. So, every effort must be made to have a good support system in place to deflect worry and troubles when they arise. That support system has to be ready to soothe all kinds of wounds and solve a multitude of problems—some are family or relationship oriented, some are health related (general or vocal), some center on career decisions, and others involve crises in scheduling or logistics. An effective support system includes every person who can help keep a singer in top shape and functioning well, mentally and physically, in good times and bad. There may not be someone who can solve the problem immediately, but just having someone reliable and sympathetic to talk to about it can be a catalyst for the release of enough emotional tension to promote a more centered approach to problem solving and allow the voice to flow naturally, releasing some of the pent-up stress.

There are several kinds of supporters that are most helpful and uplifting to a performing artist. I call them the cheerleaders, the counselors, the confidants, and the CEOs. Occasionally, singers get lucky and find one or two people who can fill all of these roles. But that is not a likely happenstance. In this case, it really will take a village to accomplish the tasks presented.

Cheerleaders can be fun, energy-boosting people to have among your support group, but they are peripheral at best and have a limited use in crisis situations or for long-term support. They rally around when things are going well, promoting your every career move. They write about all of your adventures on social media, tell all of their friends about what you are doing, and can help to bring in a bigger audience for your next event. A few of them might even get beyond their pompom-waving, tweeting status to a more personal relationship with a singer, one in which actual meaningful conversations can take place. But I wouldn't count on them in a pinch. They tend to be short-lived, fair-weather friends. Far too often, when things start to go awry, their fickle nature and shallowness take over, and they are on to the next BFF, leaving you in the dust with the last discarded version of a smart phone. So, they are not the kind of supporters that you need to call in the middle of the night when stuck in some hotel room all alone in the wrong city, having had your luggage lost by the airlines and worried that you will miss your performance date or have nothing to wear. A singer can make good use of this type of cheerleader relationship with casual friends and career followers because they are really good at spreading the word about upcoming performances, appearances, and interviews or new recordings that you have made. Unfortunately, some performers give this group of supporters too much attention, importance, and energy and never get around to making lasting connections with reliable people who will be there in a time of need.

All singers need to establish secure relationships with the finest professional advice givers they can find in their field—counselors of many kinds. Knowledgeable and caring teachers, coaches, doctors, and other professionals who give helpful advice fall into this category of counselors and are worth their weight in gold to a performing artist. It is always best if a vocalist can get references from other singers for possible counselors from whom they will seek advice on career or health issues. Word of mouth and the personal experiences of others in the vocal arts are excellent ways to begin the process and discern if the public persona of a professional advisor is accurate or not. Publicity in magazines or newspapers should not be used as the sole reason to choose a voice teacher, coach, or doctor. Anyone can create an advertisement that makes him or her sound like a much-sought-after and appropriate expert, when the opposite is true.

Once a possible counselor has been identified, the singer should do a good bit of research on any person who has been recommended and meet with him or her to see if personalities click. Even if your best friend thinks a certain doctor or voice teacher is the greatest thing since sliced cheese, that does not mean such a person is the right one for you. Several years ago, I was searching for a specialist in thyroid disorders, since mine had decided to die—my thyroid, that is. One of my friends, who had a similar problem, told me about her doctor, speaking of him in terms that might be found in descriptions of Nobel Prize winners. So, I looked him up and, being duly impressed with what I read, made an appointment, drove a good distance to see him in another city, and waited patiently for him to appear almost two hours after my appointed time. A few minutes after I was shown into his office, he walked through the door, threw some papers on his desk, and turned to his computer. I still don't remember if he actually greeted me. For the next fifteen minutes, he asked me questions while typing, never looking at me once. His tone was impersonal; he questioned my every opinion and rebuked me for not coming to see him sooner, since he was an authority. I was stunned, and I disliked him immediately. So, when he finally looked up from his computer and told me to make another appointment in a month, I said, "No, thank you. I will not be back." I knew that he was not the right health counselor for me, and I kept searching until I found a more caring and attentive expert, one that I knew I could count on for good advice and one that would be able to identify me in a line-up.

Once you have found the perfect counselors, no matter the field of expertise, it is important to establish an ongoing relationship with them before you end up in a crisis situation and need their advice about some physical or vocal problem you are experiencing while performing in a distant city. These kinds of things do happen. Those with chronic illnesses must pay particular attention to this if they hope to maintain any kind of regular performance schedule and feel confident that they will be able to keep on track.

Many years ago I had a lingering health problem that required numerous doctor visits. In the midst of that, I was engaged to sing on a new music festival in Boston. I felt fine when I left home, but my health problem flared up again so dramatically that I became quite drained and fatigued by it as the day of performance approached. I grew quite worried that I would not have the energy or the stamina to get through the performance. At that time in my life, I had an established doctor-patient relationship with a wonderful physician, the old-fashioned type who spent time talking with his patients and getting to know them and who reached for the prescription pad only after all other forms of therapy were tried. He knew that I was a singer and often asked me about my performances. He also told me that I could always call him if I needed his help, wherever I was. Fortunately, the only time I felt I had to do that was during this Boston trip. The day before the concert, I stayed in bed until noon, and by afternoon, my nerves were raw because of worry about my health. So, I decided that I needed to hear a reassuring voice with any advice that could get me through this performance without falling over. I called this doctor in my hometown. He came on the line immediately and spent ten minutes talking with me about how I felt, suggesting what I might do to feel better, and telling me what to do in case none of that worked. Just the sound of his voice calmed me down. He did give me some useful suggestions, but there was really not much he could do from a distance except reassure me that I was a strong person and remind me that with some previously successful remedies and positive thinking, I could will myself through it. And I did. I'm convinced that I would not have fared as well if I had not had this wise counselor when I needed him most.

When you choose a health care specialist, it is most important to have a physician who knows you well, understands your particular health issues, knows about any allergies you have to medications, and is careful that any medications you are taking do not negatively affect your vocal performance. I have discovered that some physicians choose to dismiss any concerns about vocal complications and prescribe things that might be temporarily or permanently harmful if taken. I don't think a singer can be too hypersensitive to this issue, since the voice must be protected to have a career. So, in my opinion, if a doctor has no interest or will not take the time to discover whether a medication might be harmful to the voice, then another doctor should be consulted. Also, if a singer has had major allergic reactions to certain medications, as I have, a good discussion with a doctor about a medication's effects—and some personal research—is warranted before taking anything, especially if it is prescribed right before a performance. Of course, there are times when singers must take medications that will affect the voice. There may be no other option. In that case, a cessation of singing might be in order until the problem for which the medication is prescribed has passed. Those performers who travel to concert engagements should carry a list of drugs, vitamins, herbs, or other substances they take on a regular basis in case they need to see a new health care specialist while away from home. It is also very important to list all known allergies to foods or drugs so that nothing will be administered that might affect you negatively. As my doctor pointed out to me, "It is hard to remember everything when you are sick and may be impossible for others to get important details about you if you are unconscious." So, performers who take medications and have allergies must be vigilant to not be injured by an innocent mistake made by a health care specialist who doesn't know you.

It is especially important for singers to have a well-established, professional, congenial, and collaborative relationship with a doctor who specializes in the care of the voice—the singing voice—if possible. Not everyone has access to voice centers such as the Vanderbilt University Voice Center, the Duke Voice Care Center, or others like them that deal specifically with the singing voice. If not, a knowledgeable ear, nose, and throat specialist who has a good reputation for treating singers would be the next best line of defense. It would be ideal if this relationship could begin when the singer is well, having no vocal problems. If possible, singers should get pictures of their vocal cords when they are healthy, for future reference. I know some professional singers who travel with a picture of their vocal cords in a glossy print or a DVD so that they will have it to show to a new doctor if vocal problems occur while they are far away from their regular specialist.

Singers are extremely sensitive and tend to worry over every slight voice change, sometimes magnifying things out of proportion. Because we cannot see our instrument, we often imagine that something is horribly wrong with the vocal cords, when they are just fine. Of course, there can be times when vocal cord injury has occurred due to illness or incorrect singing habits. So, it is good to have a voice professional available and ready for reassurance or to diagnose a problem when lingering doubt becomes anxiety and vocal dysfunction.

Sympathetic and effective voice teachers and coaches are vital to a performer's mental and vocal stability and remain as counselors long after the singer's student days, being frequently called on for advice as a singer matures. They are a central part of any performer's training and continued success. I have already discussed in an earlier chapter the desirable characteristics of these very important people as a singer begins training the voice and establishing one's career. But this relationship may be lifelong for many performers. Many mature singers continue to see voice teachers and coaches for fine-tuning of their vocal instrument, psychological bolstering, and general professional advice throughout their career.

Everyone needs to have another set of ears on a periodic basis, no matter how many years you have been on the boards, because we all fall into bad habits without realizing it. Also, as the voice ages, it can take on qualities that may seem substantially different from those heard when the voice was younger. These natural changes can worry or confuse a singer. So, it is good to have other people—who know you well—listen to you sing periodically to make sure that you haven't fallen into some vocal abyss without an escape ladder.

I have used three people over the years to be my external ears: Louis Nicholas, my doctoral work voice teacher; Patsy Wade, who has been my accompanist since I was twenty-six; and my husband, George Mabry—conductor, singer, and voice teacher. As I established my career and matured into my thirties, I found it reassuring and helpful to sing periodically for Louis Nicholas, who knew my voice inside and out. He caught every bad habit I wanted to revisit and made excellent suggestions for interpretation and vocal coloration that were useful additions to my performing style. One day after a coaching session, he said, "Sharon, I've told you everything I know. I don't have anything else to say. Don't come back for a lesson; let's just talk from now on." And we did, until he passed away a few years ago. That's the sign of a great teacher, one who knows when the student needs to move on and who doesn't try to hold on too long. Patsy and George have listened carefully and been a sounding board for all of my performances since then, giving wonderful advice. I told each of them early on that I wanted them to make sure that if I started to sound really old or do something strange or uncharacteristic with my voice to please let me know, since singers don't always recognize their own faults. They have been great counselors, pointing out when I'm making some sound or choosing to sing some piece that just doesn't suit me. I'm still waiting to see if they will really tell me when I sound old. That will be the true test.

All performers must learn to deal with the stress of this demanding profession in an effective manner. So, counselors, practitioners, and advisors of various kinds must be found who can help a singer deal with stress and its symptoms. A failure to do so can cause physical illness, energy depletion, psychological problems, and even vocal production difficulties that affect a single performance or an entire career. Some singers cope with stress better than others, perhaps due to inherent personality characteristics or because they have naturally developed coping methods that are effective. However, many singers struggle to find stress relievers, and they need assistance to do so. This is where qualified counselors of various kinds can be helpful.

I have a soprano friend who says that she would be lost without a talk therapist with whom she discusses personal issues and learns relaxation techniques; a nutritionist who plans her meals, since potato chips are her go-to food; a financial advisor who clears her mind of worries about her paycheck; a yoga instructor who teaches her how to meditate while getting her body in shape; a massage therapist who uses cranial sacral therapy to alleviate her TMJ problems; and a healing-touch therapist who smooths out her mangled energy fields. She believes that all of these counselors have helped her to be in top performance mode for many years and that without them she would have imploded long ago. Each of them has played an important part in the destressing of this very fine performer. So, I say, if it makes you happy, it doesn't matter how many counselors it takes to get you on the stage. If it works, then do it. The results are the most important thing.

Other singers may not need all of the counselors mentioned so far. Some get by with a twenty-minute daily meditation session, a few short breathing techniques, a five-mile run every afternoon, a tai chi or yoga class every few days, or a few laps around the pool. Those kinds of activities may involve a trainer or teacher but perhaps not. It doesn't matter what kind of activities work or how much time they require to keep excess stress in check. All that matters is that each singer must find the right way to do it and use any experienced, reputable, agreeable counselors available to help with the process.

The third type of person that performers need to have in their entourage of career boosters is at least one confidant—two or three, if possible. These people must be those with whom you can discuss problems and private, personal matters without fear that they will go public after talking with you. It is obvious in today's world that many performers do not have the ear of a sympathetic and caring confidant. Instead, they feel the need to blurt out the most personal issues over social media of all kinds, getting reactions from thousands, perhaps millions, of people in ways they never expected. This method of problem solving and soul-searching tends to end badly for the artist. Any negative reactions could become a personal landfill of verbal garbage that is of no use. A barrage of mostly critical, seldom helpful suggestions can cause the artist to withdraw from everyone, unable to make decisions wisely and feeling more cut off from friends and family than ever. It reminds me of the few times I watched the television show *The Price Is Right*. Contestants seem to become unsure and find it hard to make an appropriate decision about which door to open, what price to choose, or which object to uncover when the audience is screaming out lots of choices. Some seem frozen and just blurt out a decision for no good reason to get the process over. The same kind of thing can happen to a performing artist who listens to the throng, instead of talking to a few trusted people—a relative, a spouse, a voice teacher, a fellow performer, or just a very good friend—who will listen without judging and keep all conversations private. Finding the right confidants is not easy, but it is necessary to develop confidence in decision making and move on when troubles or complications interrupt an otherwise smooth-running career.

Finally, every performer needs a CEO—a personal assistant, someone who can help organize the details of a singer's life and career. To develop a well-oiled performance life, make a list of all the things you need to get done to reach your performance goals and manage your personal life. It should include everything that will keep you going on a daily basis, take your mind off nagging problems, eliminate extraneous interruptions that have nothing to do with singing, and make your life easier and more enjoyable while pursuing a career. Then, be realistic and decide what items on that list you can do yourself. Once that is done, whatever is left will have to be done by someone else, perhaps a personal assistant or someone in your family who is willing to support your career with time spent on details.

This kind of person can be instrumental in creating an existence for the singer that allows him or her to live the life one imagines and to enjoy it without undue stress and worry. In other words, you need a personal assistant of some kind if you are not good at doing this yourself. Most performers do not have artist management, are not on the roster of an agency, and do not have representation by an individual that might make many of the specific arrangements for upcoming concert engagements. Some of those artists do a lot of their own legwork in the pursuit of a career.

Most performers, especially those just starting out, schedule their own auditions and do the travel planning and publicity development themselves, or they find a person who can do it for them. Some singers are natural organizers, while others have no sense of organization at all. In the latter case, it is imperative to find someone who can do it for you. That person could be a coworker or friend who is good at organization and needs a little extra cash or someone with an outgoing personality who knows your work well and can help develop publicity materials that sell you to possible employers or venues and get auditions for you that are most beneficial. It really depends on what kind of personal assistant you need: one that just does research for you, one that sets up auditions, one that keeps your schedules, one that develops publicity in print or on the web, or one that is a good personal shopper and can do all the little things that you don't have time to do. Whatever the need, it is important to address this crucial element of performance life so that you don't end up spending all of your time worrying about details and schedules and have no time to prepare for the actual performance. I have listed several books for your consideration at the end of this volume that will help with this kind of issue.

TOAST YOUR HOSTS

There is another group of very important people that all singers encounter as they travel around the world for auditions and concert dates—they are the hosts. Where would we be without them? They are those generous people who put us up in their homes for a day or a month while we're soloing with the local orchestra, touring with a choral group, auditioning for a regional musical theatre company, singing in a small opera production in the middle of nowhere, or giving a recital at a university. They are the ones who pick us up at airports, run errands for us, make our breakfasts, drive us to rehearsals, make sure that the programs are printed, shower us with chocolate and flowers when the performance is over, and cater to our needs, no matter how strange they may be. They also save us a lot of money that we might have to spend on all of these services if not for their kindness. They manage—in small and enormous ways—to make a performer's life move more smoothly when on the road for concerts and guest appearances. We must never take them for granted. Rather, they must be thanked profusely and cherished for the time and effort they give for our benefit.

It is important to strike a balance between the artist's desire to have one's needs met and the invasion and disruption of the host's daily life. After all, the artist and host may have nothing in common as to lifestyle. So, care must be taken to respect the host's normal routine, privacy, and premises while staying for any length of time. For instance, I am aware of an incident in which a host offered to house a singer and her accompanist for three days while they were in town for a concert and some master classes. She had been informed of a few simple food requirements but had no idea that the singer would want to practice yoga in the middle of her living room. This was problematic since the singer had decided to do this workout without any clothes on, except barely-there underwear just at the time the host's husband was to arrive home from work. When the surprised host asked the singer to cease due to the impending arrival of her husband, the singer remarked that he wouldn't bother her, and she made no effort to do so until the accompanist got involved and suggested that she get herself upstairs. The singer did so reluctantly, as if it was an inconvenience to comply with the host's wishes. This particular singer must have decided to make the host's home her own, take the exhibition-ism of her life as a performer to another level, and relegate the host's life to the back burner. This kind of treatment of hosts can cause real prob-lems for the artist in the long term. Actions such as these can be transmit-ted to contracting organizations and cause future problems in finding a host for the artist. If there are major problems in communication or differ-ences that cannot be resolved, the artist or the host may have to request a change in accommodations.

It is a good idea to try to get the names and contact information for the people who will host you so that you can speak with them personally before your visit to thank them and let them know of special needs. For hosts to provide services that will be helpful and considerate, every per-forming artist should give them accurate information about personal preferences and schedule requirements; that way, the hosts can be pre-pared for anything unusual and know when and where they are expected to transport or collect the artist from rehearsals or interviews. They may not have received this information from the contracting source, so to assume that would be a mistake.

Many artists have allergies to certain foods—peanuts, wheat, milk products—and may require special diets. They may also have sensitiv-ities to other substances that cause a problem when traveling, such as perfumes and down used for bedding. I have two major food issues. First, I must avoid milk products. Not only do they make me physically sick, but my voice becomes breathy and resembles the sound of a dying exhaust fan after I eat the slightest bit of cheese. So, it is imperative that I do not have milk products of any kind right before a performance. Since most of the people who have hosted me in my travels over the years seem to prefer foods that contain lots of cream and cheese, my special milk problem caused them to have to avoid their usual routine when they prepared food for me. That is certainly an inconvenience for them but a necessary one if they are to be my host. Second, I have to have lots of protein in my diet, especially at breakfast, or I become a zombie, have no energy, and find it difficult to function. So, the hosts who do not eat meat or eat only fruit and cereal for breakfast had to provide something quite different for my visit. I always tried to make sure that hosts were aware of my particular food issues long before I arrived so that they would not be caught unaware and have to scramble at the last minute to prepare food that I could eat.

We singers encounter many kinds of hosts when we are traveling. Sometimes they are people we meet for only one occasion and never see again. But others are people who already know us, perhaps are congenial acquaintances, but have never hosted us in their homes or catered to our every need while we stayed at a nearby hotel. In either case, the host can become a longtime friend after the visit or, if it doesn't go well, an enemy. So, it is vital that a good relationship be developed while invading someone's home or routine.

Over a long career, I have encountered many memorable hosts that I recall with great fondness. There was the lively, most delightful tenor—Clifton Ware—who picked me up at the airport in Minneapolis for a three-day stay where I sang and lectured at the University of Minnesota. When I arrived at the pickup spot after landing, I had no problem finding him even though there were dozens of cars driving by, because he was circling the parking lot with my name on a large sign sticking through the sunroof of his car. So, I knew that my stay was going to be lots of fun, and it was.

Another host I'll never forget is Mary Ragland, the founder of the Nashville Opera. She hosted me in 1985 during a series of snowstorms—It rarely does that in Nashville. I had been contracted to sing Lola in Nashville Opera's performances of *Cavalleria Rusticana*. I lived only forty miles away and had planned to drive back and forth for the rehearsals and performances, but that changed when we suddenly got nine inches of snow, either closing the roads or making them impossible to maneuver from Clarksville. So, she housed the leading soprano (Santuzza), who was from Memphis, and me for two weeks while it kept snowing. Mary lived alone in a large house that had a private wing on either end. The soprano and I were each given a wing for the duration of the stay. Mine had a lovely bedroom, bath, and sitting area. Every morning we met Mary in the kitchen to talk about life, music, the arts, and how much she loved opera—she was a trained soprano with a degree from Juilliard—all while she served biscuits, bacon, and special homemade jam that was unbelievably delicious. I don't know her exact age at the time, but she was approaching seventy. One morning, I looked out my window toward her long winding driveway, where my car had been stalled in several inches of snow and left parked halfway up the hill. I could see someone shoveling the snow from around the tires and thought that it was probably a worker who did things around the house. But after a few minutes, I realized it was Mary in a big coat, boots, and furry hat. I couldn't believe it and was worried that she might hurt herself. But a short time later, when I went down to the kitchen for breakfast, she bounced in and announced that my tires were now cleared and that I should be able to get the car the rest of the way up the hill, which I did. That is some kind of unforgettable host!

There are occasions when an artist finds it difficult to adjust to accommodations provided by a host. It may be impossible to know that those conditions exist until you arrive at the location. Rather than suffer through it, sometimes it's best to cut and run.

One of the strangest occurrences in my touring history came about when Patsy Wade and I traveled to a university on the East Coast for a concert that was for university students and community combined. The local organizer had arranged for us to stay at the university's historic guesthouse, which sounded like a great idea at the time. However, when we arrived there, we discovered several disturbing things about it, not unlike one of those grainy movies that scare the living daylights out of you on Halloween.

First of all, the rather large, somewhat dark house had floors that creaked, and it was being renovated downstairs, with workmen coming in and out. The kitchen was mostly dismantled. We were shown to two large bedrooms filled with beautiful antiques and a bath on the top floor. Our local host told us that we would be alone at the house, since there was no caretaker and no one else was staying there. And by the way, there was a problem with the back door locks—there were none, since the workmen had not fixed those yet. That made me a bit nervous when we heard the train going down the track right behind the house, which could bring anyone to our unlocked back door. After thanking our host, who— seemingly unconcerned about the circumstances—left us to unpack and settle in, we talked about what might be done to keep that back door closed. We were already feeling nervous and unsafe. But we went on upstairs, Patsy to her room and I to mine. A few minutes later, she appeared at my door and said, "I've decided to sleep on the sofa on the landing instead of that bedroom." When I asked why, she said, "There's a ghost in there and I just can't sleep in that bed. I'll be alright on the landing." She was not kidding. I have always known that Patsy is psychic when it comes to our collaborative performing, but I guess it goes deeper. At that point, all of the negatives made us both want to escape, and I certainly wasn't going to have her sleep on a sofa. Fortunately, I had my own car, so I called a well-known inn that was just a few miles away and was lucky enough to get a wonderful room for us.

Being the traditional Southerners that we are—taught to please people at all cost—we felt terrible that we were shunning the hospitality of the guesthouse that they were providing. So, rather than complain and ask to be moved, we left a few clothes there, worried that they might think badly of us, got in my car and drove to the inn, had a wonderful dinner, and spent an enjoyable evening. We went back to the ghost house the next day—which by now reeked of fresh paint, as the painters had arrived early in the morning—to change clothes for the concert but went right back to the inn following it, telling our host that we had decided to stay there on the final night since it was closer to the interstate. I have no idea if our host knew of our adventure. We never spoke of it. But no one should stay in a place where one does not feel safe or that causes mental distress.

Other kinds of host problems can cause a performer to have a hard time coping with an uncomfortable situation. I recall one host who generously chauffeured us everywhere, but his cologne was stifling and caused horrible sneezing attacks for my accompanist and me. Another host invited several relatives over, without notice, to "meet the artists" two hours before the concert just as we were getting dressed. There were the scratchy, hot, flannel sheets that gave me hives at a host's home in the frozen north. One host talked incessantly for two days, even through the bathroom door while I was trying to get ready for bed—seeming to require constant interaction. Then there was the host who definitely had a hoarding problem. The entire house was stacked up to the tops of the windows with books, CDs, reel-to-reel tapes, newspapers, and other items, making one feel claustrophobic. Fortunately, the room I stayed in was less cluttered, so I just cleared out some of the items from around my bed, moved them over into a corner closet, and made room to breathe. It was doable, so I stayed.

Another host problem comes up more often than one would expect. Once in a while, hosts assume that they can be part of all of your activities, and so they want to attend rehearsals, interviews, and social events to which they have not been invited. This is a sticky, bothersome situation and one that needs to be addressed up front if possible. Rehearsals and interviews are often closed to outsiders. I have a tenor friend who told me of one occasion several years ago when his host drove him to a rehearsal, walked into the auditorium as if she had been invited, sat down, and created a scene when she was asked to leave by the concert manager. She became so irate that she didn't attend the concert, and the atmosphere at her home was less than pleasant during the rest of his stay, since she blamed him for the problem. This kind of situation might be avoided if, when engaged for an event, you try to find out from the organizers what obligations you have to your host concerning your activities. It would be best if the organizers can spell out the rules to your hosts before you arrive so that they will not make assumptions about inclusion in activities for which they have not been invited.

Though there can be occasional problems that occur when relying on hosts during performance-related travel, the tremendous care and generosity that are shown by them must be acknowledged. Even though the traditional rules of etiquette have slipped in this digital-interaction, quick-reply age, they still apply and are being brought back by books on the subject. So, look your hosts in the eye and express your appreciation; be polite and courteous; smile occasionally and talk to them cordially; and send flowers or a handwritten thank-you note—not a one-line e-mail—after you leave. Try to keep complaints to a minimum, but let the hosts know, as gently as possible, if there are problems that are causing you distress. Finally, always try to leave your accommodations in the same condition in which you found them and your host with the best impression you can muster.

* * *

REMINDERS!

- All performers need advocates to succeed.
- Seek out collaborators to expand a career; avoid isolation.
- Notice if the personality, temperament, and lifestyle of possible collaborators match your own.
- Find collaborators who have similar skill levels and musical ideas and will tolerate eccentricities.
- Singers and accompanists should have mutual respect and not waste each other's time.
- Connect with creative artists outside your field of expertise.
- Create your own performance opportunities, and don't wait to be discovered.
- Develop a support system of people you can trust for advice—not fawning fans.
- Find cheerleaders, counselors, confidants, and CEOs to bolster your career.
- Show gratitude to generous hosts by being courteous and expressing appreciation for their efforts.

SEVEN

Create the Life You Imagine

It is difficult to build a career in performance without a dream, a vision, an idea, or a spark of creativity that ignites the fire of desire to get up on a stage and display your art for the public. Without the kindling, the fire may fizzle due to a lack of inspiration and aspiration needed to achieve lofty goals. Not everyone craves the goal of being a performer enough to withstand all the cumulative stress and serendipity of a performer's life. Sometimes, the romanticized life of a performer is all that drives a person to seek out the profession. That alone is not nearly enough. If singers do not prepare, plan, and spend quality time investigating all that is involved in a performer's life, they may find out too late—and with harsh realization—that it is not the life for them.

Once the preparation, planning, and investigating have been done and the decision has been made to pursue a performing career, other factors come into play that have to be addressed. Realistically, a performer's existence can be overwhelming at times, especially if attention has not been paid to the creation of a harmonious lifestyle and mind-set that can withstand all kinds of pressures while being pulled in several directions at once—continuing to develop skills through practice, making important career contacts, sorting out criticism and compliments from all sides, learning new repertoire, perhaps working at a part-time job, and having responsibilities outside the career itself.

Assuming that the singer possesses adequate vocal skills and musical ability, success in this type of career requires good coping techniques built on a positive self-image, a clear delineation of career goals, and both short-term and long-range planning. Without these important building blocks, the daily life of a performer can become burdensome, lack personal and professional satisfaction, and cause anxiety due to a chaotic inner and outer life. A career is more likely to thrive and become a joyful

adventure if the performer approaches what can be a complicated existence with a positive attitude, creates long-term goals, cultivates good
interpersonal relationships, continues to seek advice and learns from experience, and becomes flexible enough to go with the flow when obstacles interfere with the best-laid plans.

As part of the career-planning process, take the quality time needed to
visualize the kind of existence that makes you feel content, then set about
constructing the life you picture, piece by piece, revisiting the vision on a
regular basis to make sure that all elements really provide a sense of
inner balance. Performers benefit from considering several topics that
help determine what they need to do in their inner and outer lives to
create the overall life they imagine. Answering the following questions is
a good start in this process:

- Where would I like to live?
- What would my ideal day look like?
- Can my self-esteem stand up to public criticism?
- What do I like to do in my free time?
- Do I want to have a life partner, perhaps children?
- How do I view the scope of my career now and in the future?
- Am I willing to travel extensively to be successful?
- How will I finance my career dreams?
- Do I have supportive people around me?
- What kinds of activities do I enjoy?
- What interests me outside the performance medium in which I am
  engaged?
- Do I want to spend time in service to my community?
- Do I have habits that affect my performing career negatively?
- Do I spend enough quality time in reflection and quietude?
- Do I practice effective techniques for relieving stress?
- Is the self-talk in my head positive or negative?
- Do I have a belief system about life that works for me?

There are many aspects of a performer's life that just happen without
much planning. Sometimes, there are chance meetings with people who
can catapult a career into overdrive. But most of the time, it is the
thoughtful planning and evaluation, inner vision, complete preparation,
and readiness of the singer that allow him or her to achieve goals and not
be deterred by negative blips in the career-building process.

PLAN FOR SUCCESS

It is quite useful to write out a plan—a list of things that need to be done
to achieve specific or general career goals—and revisit it every few
months or once a year to see if it still excites you when you visualize what

might happen to your life if that plan really comes to pass. You don't have to be stuck to the plan. It can morph into something slightly different, but at least you have given thought to what you would like to do with the rest of your life and have mapped out ways in which you might get to your goal.

I've always been a planner. It seems to be a natural part of my personality, a characteristic that appeared early in life. If my parents were planners, it was not evident to me—which caused me a good bit of distress. Their seeming lack of concern about sticking to predetermined schedules for trips and other events drove me crazy. So, even as a young child, I kept a little date book marked with upcoming recitals, civic club performances, rehearsals, parties, or other events that I was to attend, and I pestered my parents daily with reminders about staying on the schedule—which probably caused them a good bit of distress.

I wouldn't call myself an obsessive planner but one that just loves to do it. Planning has always been fun for me and quite helpful in visualizing and creating excitement about upcoming events. For example, fifteen minutes before my wedding, I was standing in the hallway outside the church sanctuary—dressed in my wedding gown—checking off items on a to-do list to make sure that everything had been done before the ceremony began. That might seem tedious to some, but it made the event even more anticipatory for me. Since that time, my penchant for planning has come in handy in professional and personal ways. I have not only planned my own professional concert engagements down to the last detail but used those skills to complete several house renovations and plan vacation trips for my family as well as for friends who know that I love to do it. So, I'm sure that one day my gravestone will read—*Sharon Mabry, The Planner*. But, seriously, it is an extremely valuable tool, one that I'm very glad to have as a natural component of my personality.

For those singers who do not possess this skill, it can be refined with practice and help from personal assistants, professionals who teach people how to organize, or books on the subject.

Start with small steps that can be accomplished easily, then eventually take more general control of daily life and career planning. Here are a few concepts that have helped me to plan well over the years:

1. Define your short-term and long-range goals.
2. Visualize what your goals will do for you.
3. Decide to pay attention to achieving your goals.
4. Assess the amount of time it will take to reach each goal.
5. Make a list of things that need to be done to reach each goal.
6. Mark off each item on the list as it is accomplished.
7. Put all items not accomplished on a previous list at the top of the new list.

8. With each step taken, congratulate yourself and say, "I'm moving forward."
9. Consider whether you need help from others to reach your goals.
10. Officially celebrate the achievement of each goal, no matter how small.
11. Revisit your original goals on a regular basis and revise if necessary.
12. Look forward to new adventures if original goals have changed.
13. Don't look back with regret on goals not achieved.
14. Don't give credence to criticism about the appropriateness of your goals.

Budding performers need to have definite career goals to move forward. Successful people tend to dream big dreams and accentuate the positives at every level of achievement. However, some big dreams, when realized, may contain unanticipated negative elements that are difficult to overcome to live a healthy, happy life. Given this possibility, young artists should thoroughly investigate all aspects of their dreams to make sure their requirements suit their personalities and desired lifestyles.

Self-analysis and career research are critical endeavors when deciding what to do with the rest of your life. This approach takes organization and planning. So, once a dream (goal) is clearly projected in the mind's eye, the performing artist must write out a plan, visualize it, explore its options, get prepared, and develop a lifestyle that will bring happiness, not dread and disappointment.

Everyone needs to get a reality check concerning whether they are really suited to their dream life. When I was a college student, the Broadway stage beckoned me. I loved everything about the musical theatre, or so I thought. I auditioned for summer stock theatre companies and worked every summer between my freshman year and the summer after graduation playing leading and secondary roles in productions at regional theatres. The experience was exciting. I made lots of friends and learned a great deal about being on the stage. But more important, I came into contact with several veteran actors who had been on the circuit for a while. I watched and listened as they discussed their travels, family situations, financial difficulties, and uncertainties about their future in the business. I talked with them about just what kind of sacrifices they had made to keep going on their way to Broadway.

All of this experience was valuable and gave me a more realistic picture of what it really meant to live the vagabond life of an aspiring musical theatre performer. By the end of my fourth summer, I knew that it was not the life for me. Though I loved the music and enjoyed every moment on the stage, I realized that I had romanticized a life in the theatre and had never considered what it really took to be successful there. More important, I discovered through self-analysis and observation of what it took to thrive in that arena that my personality and sensibility did not suit that lifestyle. I knew that I needed a regular routine, a home base, and plenty of outside encouragement to succeed as a musician. And though I liked to travel, I didn't want to live out of a suitcase indefinitely. I realized that I was not prepared to cope with the uncertainty of the profession. I know now that my decision to go in another direction was the correct one because it led me to other talents that developed into the satisfying career that I have enjoyed in teaching, professional classical singing, and writing.

A major part of the career-planning process involves immersion in the vocal art to which you aspire. For a career plan to become reality, it is necessary for a singer to become familiar with the chosen performance genre's stylistic features, performance opportunities, and most successful artists. If singers want to sing on Broadway or at the Metropolitan Opera, then they must listen to professional recordings of every musical or opera they can get their hands on, become familiar with past and present lauded performers in the genre, attend live performances when possible, and study every aspect of that genre to know whether their particular talents suit it. This does not mean that a young singer should set out to imitate famous performers; rather, they should be used as inspirational examples of what is the finest of the art.

It is folly to assume that one has what it takes to be successful in singing a particular musical style if unfamiliar with its characteristics or with those who have been notable performing it. If a singer has no idea of the vocal style, sound quality, and performance requirements for the profession to which she or he aspires, it is difficult to develop confidence or compete with others who will be more attuned to its norms and requirements. As a teacher of aspiring performers, I am often struck by how little discriminating research they have done to prepare for the career they have chosen. A lack of immersion in the subject can result in only a faint picture of what it really takes to achieve success as a performer. Some young singers have slim knowledge of outstanding performers in the field and have given little listening time to highly rated recordings of their work. In the olden days—before the advent of multitudinous web choices for performance presentations—a recording that one purchased was generally of a professional-level performance, one that could be admired and may have received critical acclaim as a valid example of artistic excellence. In today's "everything goes public" world of Internet performances, one has to search carefully for those excerpts that are truly professional and characteristic of any genre, since the web is cluttered with musical presentations that should not be used as performance goals for which an upcoming singer ought to strive. Unfortunately, with or without good advice from a teacher or coach, naïve young singers may not recognize professional names as ideal examples of their art, or they may ignore advice on the subject and listen only to others who provide less-than-stellar examples. This problem seems to be getting worse, since I hear the same complaint from many of my voice teacher colleagues.

Recently, I chatted with a junior-level vocal performance major—an excellent student, academically—who shared her dreams of becoming an opera singer. As we talked, it became obvious that she was not aware of very many recorded examples of professional opera singers, especially those with her voice type. She had listened—only once—to two singers that had been recommended by her voice teacher but could name no one else nor any opera roles that might suit her voice. Instead, she spoke excitedly of several short YouTube viewings of three familiar arias that she had sung recently. I went with her to my computer, where she pointed them out so that I could hear the ones she liked best. Unfortunately, most were of young singers like herself, who were recorded in college performances or studio situations. It was obvious that some had less formal training and ability than she and were not within sight of a professional-level performance. Yet, she seemed perfectly happy with these renditions as gospel for the art of opera singing. That kind of hit or miss—accept anything that goes over the airwaves—research and familiarity with the profession is not helpful in the long run and is unlikely to raise the singer's level of artistic ability. So, it is imperative that singers engage in appropriate discriminating research and seek out the most successful, highly praised performers in whatever musical genre they choose as ideal models.

DEVELOP A WORKABLE LIFESTYLE

Singers have to make a living. Some who wish to perform full-time are lucky enough to be able to make a good living at that one profession without taking on other kinds of jobs. However, many—especially those just starting out—find that they must supplement their performing career with other jobs that bring in money. Young singers often seek out part-time jobs in retail, restaurant service, or computer technology that will allow them time off for auditions and performance engagements. They may decide to teach a few voice students at home or for an area arts academy or university. That kind of part-time work added to a performance career is quite doable unless both careers start to take on full-time status. When that occurs, the combined demands may be too much to handle, causing physical and mental distress and an inability to be consistently prepared and achieve goals in either area.

Some singers choose to inhabit a dual-career lifestyle. They do this for many reasons—intellectual interests and opportunities that build on an alternate expertise, interests that are complementary to the performing medium, or the need for a release from the stress of performing. If the two careers are complementary, then it is possible that the alternate career could enhance the development of the performance realm. If they are not complementary, then the singer's time and attention may be drastically skewed in a direction that will take too much time and attention from performing, causing the singer to give less and less preparation detail to the performance career. Though the pursuit of two careers at once can be exciting and energizing and bring more opportunities for financial gain, professional contacts, and reputation enhancement, it can cause serious problems for the performer. If the singer finds that, due to a dual-career lifestyle, there is no time to rest, ponder, study musical scores, or practice, then something must be done about this problem or performances will suffer. These all-consuming attributes of having a dual career can affect the voice and performance in negative ways. So, careful thought, soul-searching, and planning must be given to this undertaking to develop a workable, enjoyable dual-career lifestyle that does not sabotage a singer's performing life.

Inhabiting the lifestyle of a dual-career professional artist requires a super-sized sense of organization and self-awareness. It is not easy wearing two giant hats, each demanding energy, concentration, study, planning, and ultimate organization to succeed. Certain personality types do well in this kind of situation, but those who find it difficult to manage stress or make decisions, who tend toward excessive worry about details, and who lack good organizational skills may find that a two-career lifestyle is not right for them. Also, to maintain a dual-career lifestyle, both careers must be equally rewarding, or one inevitably gets pushed to the back burner, begins to receive less attention, and finally fades due to a lack of attention. The result of an inability to live a dual-career lifestyle, happily and smoothly, can be fatal to a performing career. If singers begin to pay more attention to their other career, do not take care of their voices properly, or let performance preparation slide, then their levels of performance will diminish, their reputation as performers will suffer, and performance anxiety may become an issue due to a lack of proper preparation and consistent practice.

One of the most commonly seen combinations for dual careers is that of the performing artist–teacher. Performing and teaching used to be thought of as mutually exclusive careers. But things have changed dramatically. The performing artist–teacher is a staple in the professional world of music making today. That old saying "Those who perform, do, and those who can't, teach" is no longer accurate and perhaps never was. Historically, many performers taught a few students here and there to make ends meet, and most teachers occasionally performed in public as professional musicians. Today, many more professional performers are choosing to teach at least part-time and are doing it with enthusiasm. It is no longer unusual to find exceptional teachers who perform on a regular basis, working at their "day jobs" in conservatories, universities, and private academies, then traveling to sing guest recitals, perform with symphony orchestras or chamber ensembles, or play roles in opera and musical theatre company productions around the country and internationally. All of this professional activity sounds exciting—and it can be— but it can also be exhausting.

These artist-teachers choose this lifestyle not only because they are fine performers who may be in demand but also because they want to stay connected to their art in the most active sense. Though every fine teacher recognizes the need to be a first-rate purveyor of information to the next generation of musicians, those who continue to perform while teaching feel a need to feed their musical souls with the thrill of music making at the highest level possible. For them, this kind of musical engagement sparks an enthusiasm for all aspects that surround it, including a desire to pass on knowledge gained to upcoming students of the art.

Any singer who decides to embark on a dual career in teaching and singing must be hypersensitive to one's own vocal, psychological, and health requirements to survive the demands of both professions. I can speak directly to the complications of that kind of lifestyle since my entire performing career has taken place while teaching full-time at the university level. Those of us who have chosen this "lunacy," as one of my colleagues put it, have done so for various reasons: creative, financial, or fear of getting bored in only one. In some cases, conservatories or universities hire professional singers to give master classes on a regular basis or teach full-time as they are approaching the final years of a performance career. This can be an exceptional opportunity for student inspiration and learning if the professional singer finds teaching to be a natural and fulfilling means of imparting gems of wisdom from a career well spent in performing, rather than a fallback occupation.

Assuming that one has the knowledge and initial enthusiasm for teaching, there are other variables to consider that can complicate the dual-career lifestyle. Teaching requires the ability to hone in on the problems and quirks of others to effect positive change in their behavior, skills, and general performance outcome. Some teachers come by that naturally and have natural EQ (emotional intelligence), while others have to work to develop it. However, it is also true that as with "mothering," some just don't have the gene for it.

Having taught a course in vocal pedagogy at the university level for more than thirty-five years and encountered singers of all talent levels among my students, I have discovered that there is no way to predict whether the best performers will turn out to be the best teachers. As part of the course requirements, each student in the class is responsible for teaching weekly private voice lessons to a beginner for the entire semester. Often, as the class progresses, the student teachers and I are surprised by their reaction to teaching. Some class participants have an obvious, immediate, and unexpectedly positive response to the idea of teaching someone else to sing, while others find that teaching is something akin to going to the dentist. I recall one student's comment to me at the end of the semester. As she turned in her final exam, she said, "I'm so glad I took this class. I now know that I never want to teach anyone to do anything. I just don't care whether they get better or not." She was a fine singer who had already won a number of accolades for her talent, including several vocal competitions. But in her case and many others, the dual career of artist-teacher should not be attempted if teaching is something that seems more tedious than rewarding. Both the teacher and the students will suffer if there is no joy in the process.

In a case such as this, either the performer ego is not able to give way to the teacher empathy needed to be successful as an artist-teacher, or the person simply has no aptitude for teaching in general. There is no shame in this. No one can be good at everything. One simply needs to find out through experience, such as taking a vocal pedagogy class or making other small attempts at teaching a few students, whether the attachment of teaching to a performance career will work for the performing artist. If not, then it is better to leave this dual-career choice to those who truly love it.

It is obvious when teachers love to teach. They talk about their students, current and past, and relate stories of what they have achieved to their colleagues. Many of my artist-teacher colleagues have expressed the same delight I have felt at learning that one of their former students has reached some desirable and respected status in the profession. These expressions of support for students under their care are a perfect example of how the performer ego of the artist-teacher has given way to the teacher empathy.

I have found it immensely rewarding to work with young singers. They have inspired me to learn new music, think about performing and teaching in enlightening ways, and work out technical issues in my own voice while fixing vocal problems they present in lessons. It has been satisfying to know that I played a positive role in their development and subsequent success as professionals.

I am certain that these attributes of the teaching professional's life have bolstered my singing career. However, trying to juggle both careers has also presented a challenge and an organizational nightmare at times. There are missed lessons to make up when you have been out of town singing with an orchestra or doing a recital coupled with two days of master classes at a university hundreds of miles away. Teaching schedules have to be made flexible so that there is time for undisturbed, quality practice when the voice is fresh. For me, that is in the morning between 9:30 and 11:00, before I talk all day while teaching classes or demonstrating tones and technique for private students.

Even if no formal practice session is planned, I always warm up my voice before embarking on a day of teaching. Many years ago, I attended a very informative master class given by Jan De Gaetani, the great

American performing artist–teacher. I implemented many ideas learned there, but one sentence she spoke still stands out for me. She talked about singers who teach and the need to always warm up the voice slowly and carefully before starting out the teaching day. She also said that no matter how old you are, always warm up the voice with the idea of finding your "little girl voice" first, rather than bullying it into motion. Due to that statement and good advice from my mentor, Louis Nicholas, I developed vocal warm-ups that are quiet, casual, based on hums and slides, and never start out with pyrotechnics. I do them while getting dressed in the morning and while driving to the university so that by the time my first student arrives, my voice will be in the proper range, will feel flexible, and will be ready to speak and sing without strain.

As a beginning teacher, I used my singing voice much more than I do now to demonstrate appropriate vocal placement and tone color to students, especially beginners. I soon realized that I was singing several hours a day and literally wearing out my own voice while training others. I was too tired, vocally, to practice my own repertoire. So, I redoubled efforts to improve my teaching skills and vocabulary for technical explanation, which allowed me to use my singing voice less. I still demonstrate proper tone and phrasing for students on a regular basis but not nearly to the extent that I once did, and I sing with my students even less right before a performance. For the aging singer, who may not be performing as often, this daily vocalization is quite helpful in keeping the instrument well oiled so that it remains flexible and fresh. It also provides energetic responses that keep the mind and body fit while doing breathing exercises, tongue twisters, and other kinds of activities with students.

Talking is hard on the voice. The voice will tire easily if the speaking tone is too low and puts pressure on the vocal mechanism. So care must be taken not to talk too much nor too loudly and to always keep the speaking voice within a medium range that is free of fry tones or crackles. My voice likes to be coaxed, not pummeled. I have always had a delicate voice and found it crucial to speak with a clear tone and in a comfortable middle register at all times, never using it to make strange, crazy unsupported sounds. That kind of vocal behavior definitely takes a toll and tires the instrument quickly. It is not something I take lightly if I have to go to a rehearsal after teaching several hours during the day. Sometimes, those end-of-day rehearsals cannot be avoided. Thus, care has to be taken to save the instrument so that it will be strong when needed. Forethought must be given to these demands so that rehearsals or performances do not suffer from a lack of planning, depleted energy, or a weak voice. It may be necessary to cancel all teaching on the day of a performance. I know some singers who cancel all teaching for a week prior to a performance. They find it impossible to sing well if the voice has been in heavy use within a few days of a concert. No two singers are alike in handling dual-career demands, and each must discover what works best in keeping the voice healthy, fresh, and ready to sing when needed.

Given the occupational stress, time constraints, work requirements, obligations, and expectations for the teaching and performing fields, it is difficult to sustain a high level of achievement in each. This type of dual career is not for the faint of heart. Only those who truly love both and feel less than whole without either should pursue such a rewarding but demanding combination career, one that is incredibly exhilarating for those who thrive in its daily opportunities for creativity.

DESIGN A BALANCED LIFE

One of the most important considerations for those who enter the performing realm is the need to fashion a harmonious inner life that will complement a workable outer lifestyle. Since the nature of the singer's inner life will eventually affect the outer life—which includes the quality and longevity of artistic performance outcomes—everything that touches a singer needs to be identified and analyzed to see if it promotes balance or is a detriment to a healthy inner life. The creation of a daily existence that allows time for oneself, as well as one's art, is essential. To be fresh and imaginative and to have the required stamina for the performance arena, a singer needs to make time for play, reflection, and the development of emotional, intellectual, and spiritual interests. A nonstop work life, without downtime for fun, relationship development, introspection, exercise, and intellectual pursuits or general curiosity, can lead to extreme stress and poor health. It can also contribute to the burnout effect that occurs when performers push themselves too long, too hard, and maintain a fast-paced lifestyle that never allows a break from the daily grind of trying to get ahead. In other words, all work and no play can be deadly for performers.

It is unrealistic to think that one can achieve a life that is perpetually happy. No two people can agree on what that means, as Dr. Andrew Weil points out in his book *Spontaneous Happiness*. Instead, it is more realistic to try to live a balanced life—one that has contentment and satisfaction filled with highs and lows—and to be able to cope with the lows in constructive ways. To find a satisfying life balance, the singer must determine any changes that need to be made in lifestyle, thought patterns, personal relationships, or day-to-day activities that are detracting from the desired goal of a contented inner life.

The development of self-awareness is crucial to the creation of a balanced life picture that includes satisfying social relationships. Daniel Goleman calls this self-awareness *EQ* in his book *Emotional Intelligence* and discusses its importance in the establishment of good relationships and a more balanced life. People like to be around those who have EQ.

They tend to make every situation, no matter how tense, calmer and less dramatic. Many performers have enough IQ and level of musical talent to make it in the performing world, but their lack of EQ can be a roadblock on the way to a satisfying career. EQ involves relating to others with empathy, being a good listener, being assertive but cooperative, and respecting other people's opinions. These characteristics help a performer to maneuver through career development, criticism, and relationship building with tools that make life move along easier. A performer who can replace frustration, impatience, and anger with compassion, flexibility, and compromise will fare better in the long run than one who butts heads, refuses to listen to the opinions of others, and confronts people who regularly appear in their path to career goals.

I have performed with many professional singers over the years and observed how they interacted with fellow performers, directors, coaches, and stage crew. Some isolate themselves totally, give no clue to their personality, talk to no one, and present only a performer's face and voice in rehearsals and performances. Others light up a room with a personality that engages those around them in delightful, inclusive conversation about subjects other than their own voice and the music at hand. Then there are those whose presence overtakes an arena by sheer brashness and force. Suddenly, every aspect of the situation seems to have been stacked against them so that it is difficult to proceed without a constant battle of wits with other performers or those in charge. Nothing seems to be going right for them. Time is wasted in trying to satisfy demands that the singer feels must be met to continue. And all conversation among participants has been stilled due to a lengthy monologue from the singer who is consumed by his or her own concerns. This singer has very little EQ and finds it hard to work within a group of people without causing distress for everyone.

Singers tend to talk a lot about themselves and their singing, perhaps too much. Some obsess about it, beginning and ending every personal interaction with stories of their vocal problems, auditions, performance conquests, and other tidbits of information that might be better left unsaid or vented with a vocal coach or counselor. These self-centered, one-way conversations can take over family life and limit interactions with potential friends, who may not be musicians and who really don't want to hear about how you sang that high note better than anyone you know or how you feel superior to the person who was chosen instead of you in the latest audition. A twenty-four-hour day that has nothing in it except thoughts about singing and career highs and lows can lead to stress, obsession, and the exclusion of other interesting subjects and people that might enter one's life. There is no doubt that a self-centered, egotistical performer who blots out everyone and everything else in life can reach the top of the professional singing world. However, this kind of self-absorption can block possibilities of developing lasting relationships and result in isolation and emotional starvation for the singer.

It is obvious that one of opera's most compelling singers, Renée Fleming, has engaged in well-spent time in performance preparation and has had an exciting and lauded career. But it is interesting that in a *20/20* television interview in January 2000, she stated that her number one goal is to live a good life. Over the years, many fine artists have expressed the sentiment that there is more to life than performing. There has to be, or else the endless hotel rooms, superficial tweets from fans, take-out meals, and constant travel will add up to very little satisfaction in the end. The time that performers spend off the stage, outside practice rooms, not teaching, not thinking about music, can be deafeningly lonely and unfulfilling if not centered on meaningful elements of a life picture that satisfies other cravings in the singer's psyche and emotional being. That life picture can involve a continuing interest in learning new things—things that have nothing to do with music: enjoyment of hobbies or sports activities, creating caring relationships with family and friends, giving back to the community through service of some kind, developing another skill (like painting or woodworking), or spending quality time in self-exploration through meditation, spiritual retreats, or introspective mind-body endeavors such as yoga or chi gong. All of these activities and ventures can contribute to a balanced inner and outer life that maintains health and well-being and can affect the voice in a positive way. Getting outside the spectrum of a constant focus on the voice will, in the long run, be good for the voice. The broadening of a singer's scope of interests and knowledge of the world outside of vocal performance can also serve to expand one's ability to more creatively express poetic and musical ideas created by others. So, becoming a more well-rounded person is a benefit to the career and to the quality of life in general.

Singers who perform must also realize that events in life will sometimes interfere with performing. When circumstances disrupt the normal performance routine to the point that the mind and voice cannot perform while experiencing physical distress, mental distraction, or emotional concern for others, decisions must be made whether to continue or take a break. Personal illness or that of a close friend or family member, a relationship crisis such as a divorce, or the death of someone close may cause a singer to take a pause in one's career to recuperate, help out with someone else's difficult situation, or grieve. All of these events are important passages that everyone deals with in life. But the singer's voice will most likely reflect the state of one's emotions, and it may be impossible to move on and sing well until closure has been felt in a particular situation. The residual tension may stay in the voice even after the crisis has passed. So, the singer should be careful to coax the voice back into action after a traumatic or energy-draining life event.

It is helpful to seek advice from many sources for ways to improve your inner life. There are numerous books on the subject. I have listed some in the back of this volume that have been helpful to me, but many more exist that may offer just the right answer for a singer's particular life situation and needs. Also, counseling from a friend or professional is a valuable source of inner sustenance. So, be proactive, read, listen, talk to other performers about what has worked for them, and observe those who seem to cope well with all aspects of the performer's life to find answers that will apply to any vacant spots in your own.

Through a long career, I have experimented with advice from many sources that have helped me to cope with stress, bolster self-confidence, and calm inner doubts and anxiety. Some suggestions were more beneficial than others. Some have become staples in my daily life, while others were transient experiments that didn't pan out or offer much improvement, lasting satisfaction, or application to my particular situation. There are several routines, habits, regimens, and attitudes that I believe are of particular importance and use for the performing artist. They have worked for me and may work for you as well.

Get rid of negative thought patterns. We are what we think. Our thoughts are a self-fulfilling prophecy of things to come. Every morning when we arise, we have the option to think something positive or something negative. That continues throughout the day. If we choose to think something negative, it will affect the way that we feel about every aspect of the day. We all have negative chatter running through our heads, but singers seem to obsess about everything: whether others like the sound of their voice, whether they will be ready for an audition in time, how they will finance their goals, whether they will hit that high note on page 3. If it can be obsessed about, it will be obsessed about because singing is such a personal art that is tied to the emotions of the performer. Some people find that the self-flagellation is there on an hourly basis, some experience it only occasionally, but getting rid of it is easier said than done. It's not just a matter of deciding one day that you will wake up and never think a negative thought about yourself or your performing ability again. Oh, if it were only that simple.

To change destructive patterns in thinking is a process that requires a plan. One of the primary elements of that plan is to create positive self-talk or self-affirmations. Positive self-talk is the kind of mental chatter that emphasizes your best qualities, skills, and characteristics. Once it gets going and is able to block out all of those destructive, worrisome thoughts, your confidence will improve, anxiety will decrease, and the enjoyment of performance events and appreciation of the achievement of goals will increase. As the repetition and use of self-affirmations become part of the subconscious, you begin to have a more positive feeling about your own capabilities, which leads to more overall confidence. I have found this to be true in my case and in the students I have taught. So, it is useful to make a list of positive affirmations that you can use as self-talk on a regular basis, making them readily available when something negative pops into your mind. These affirmations could deal with your skills as a performer, health and wellness, musical preparation, the performance situation itself, or any area that seems to prevent you from going forward with confidence. It is important that the positive self-talk not be associated with comparison to other performers, such as *I sing better than anyone in this competition.* That kind of affirmation is not helpful and will cause confidence problems if someone else wins. I refer to the use of self-talk in other parts of this book (see chapter 3). Positive self-talk has helped me immensely to maneuver through numerous difficult times when health issues, logistical nightmares, or general stress was threatening to take its toll on my performance capabilities. The affirmations I have relied on most are as follows:

> *I am well prepared.*
> *I enjoy being on the stage.*
> *I feel calm and relaxed.*
> *I have an excellent memory.*
> *I am enjoying this process.*
> *I am making progress.*
> *I am strong and successful.*
> *I can get through difficult situations.*
> *I love this music.*
> *I have a strong support system.*
> *I am confident in my ability.*

Don't live in the past. Singers are prone to obsess over past mistakes or what they perceive as less-than-desirable performance outcomes, ones that may have occurred years before but keep resurfacing as negative self-talk right before each performance. In my personal experience and in dealing with other singers who experience performance blips, most of these situations were really minor happenings that have been blown out of proportion in the singer's mind. Some singers project slight errors in words and musical entrances and other performance miscues as personal defects that define them as performers. They see themselves as forever having flaws that cannot be improved on. This is a very destructive mind-set based on negative events that may have happened in the past and, though they no longer apply, are still very much in the present for the performer who continues to obsess about them. Those who live in the past are stuck, doomed to repeat old habits, and reminisce incessantly about past shortcomings, missing out on the enjoyment of what is happening at any given moment. To be intellectually and emotionally present for each performance, it is essential to learn to live in the now, not in the past. The elimination of negative mental chatter is essential to promoting healthy singing and the enjoyment of performing. The development of positive self-talk and the practice of mindful meditation (sitting quietly for a few minutes, paying attention to the breath, becoming aware of one's body, acknowledging thoughts and sensations without assigning them as pleasant or unpleasant) are two tools that have been used by many singers to get rid of preoccupation with past events that had faults of some kind. Yoga, the practice of the Alexander Technique, tai chi, breathing exercises, and running are other effective means of diverting the mind from obsessive thinking. I have found several of these techniques to be useful—especially tai chi, mindful meditation, and breathing exercises—to increase concentration and help calm the brain so that it can focus on the performance at hand. Also, developing a sense of humor about past errors, forgiving yourself for making them too important in your life, and concentrating on positive elements of the work in which you are currently engaged help to divert the mind from the past. Learning to let go of actual hurtful, embarrassing, or career-changing events is more difficult to achieve if a sustained pattern of mental and emotional abuse by voice teachers or others has occurred. In this case, professional help is warranted and necessary—perhaps psychological counseling is needed or a different voice teacher or coach who is more positive in approach—to develop a more positive approach to performance and live in the present.

Write it all down. One of the most beneficial pieces of advice I ever received about developing a sense of self, monitoring vocal and musical progress, and ridding the mind of stress was suggested by a singer friend who kept a daily journal. She had done this for years and recommended it as a concrete way for me to visualize just where I had been, where I might go, and what I was thinking as I went on my way. So, I took her advice and started doing that early in my career. It has been extremely useful and has helped me to vent my fears and shape my dreams without doing it publicly. I started small, stating goals and wishes, or writing down a few occurrences that stood out as major events that changed my day in some way. But, eventually, I expanded the journal to include many kinds of things: a list of short-term and long-range goals; names of friends who crossed my path or came to my aid; performance contacts who were helpful; a list of things for which I was grateful; assessments of practice sessions, rehearsals, and performances; fears and how I might handle them; books that had been helpful in some way; and a final statement to project me on to the coming day. My favorite one is "I will survive and thrive!" I don't write about the same subjects every day; however, I have settled on a few calming, positive affirmations that I continue to write in the journal on a regular basis. A journal of daily living can take any form. It does not have to be at all like the one I've just described. It can contain statements about personal satisfaction, worries, lines of poetry, sketches, future plans, or free-flowing descriptions of life as it is being experienced. One of my friends uses her journal to write short stories that are taken from her performance experiences. The most important aspect of this practice of writing down your feelings and experiences is not to be self-conscious or try to abide by any universal rules of journaling to have a good journaling experience. Fashion a journal that works for you, knowing that you can change it as you please.

Learn to disengage. Every performer has to have some recuperative downtime, time to just *be*, when words such as *frantic, busy,* and *schedule* can take a backseat to *relaxation, play,* and *freedom.* In such an exhibitionist profession, it is difficult for some personality types to come to grips with solitude. I have a hard time relaxing and have to work at it. I envy those who easily spend an afternoon languidly relaxing by the pool without any sense of guilt at doing so. If I sit down and take a break, shortly I start to feel that I should be doing something constructive—practicing, grading papers, reorganizing a closet, reading a new vocal pedagogy book, doing laundry, or answering e-mails. It doesn't really matter whether the task concerns my profession or simply keeps my household going.

It is a pattern learned from childhood and one that is hard to break. Each singer must decide for oneself what kinds of activities and regimens can be added or subtracted from life to disengage and bring about the kind of atmosphere needed to improve its overall quality. I've experimented with many different ideas for physical and mental diversion and have found several that work well for me—ways to leave teaching, performing, and professional life behind for a while to let my mind disengage from the constant need to drive full steam ahead. Tai chi has been a lifesaver. Tai chi is a gentle, graceful form of exercise that has been called "meditation in motion" and promotes general health, according to the Mayo Clinic and other health centers. I started learning it during a period of severe physical illness to build up my energy, and it has remained a staple of my routine for stress relief and disengagement from everyday pressures. Callanetics—amazing, slow, gentle, stretching exercises—have also been important in keeping my nonathletic body in shape for singing and life in general. I started doing them to strengthen my weak back in the mid-eighties at the suggestion of a singer friend, and I still do them, religiously, every morning and evening to stay limber and relaxed as I age. There are two breathing exercises that enable me to calm my mind, get in touch with natural body energy, and feel that my breath is balanced and flowing freely each morning and evening. Since I teach these exercises to my voice students, I often do them at other times during the day as demonstration:

> *Exercise 1:* Breathe in through the nose for four counts, hold the breath for seven counts, and breathe out through the mouth for eight counts; repeat four to seven times. This one is particularly useful to calm jitters or prepare the body and mind just before going to bed.

Exercise 2: Breathe in on a count of five, hold for five, breathe out for five. Repeat for six, seven, eight, nine, and ten counts. This one works well in the morning to get oxygen into the brain and get the day started with energy.

The *relaxation response exercise,* as taught to me years ago by one of my physicians, has also been extremely helpful to relax tense muscles after a tiring day of teaching, long rehearsals, or plane flights. To begin, sit in a quiet place. Pay attention to your breathing for a minute or so. Then direct your attention to the bottom of your feet and begin to relax your body from the bottom up, one bit at a time, starting with the soles of your feet and moving up through the ankles, legs, knees, thighs, pelvis, waist, diaphragm area, chest, shoulders, upper arms, elbows, wrists, hands, fingers, front of neck, back of neck, jaw, ears, face, forehead, and scalp until every muscle seems relaxed. Then go back and pay attention to any place in the body that still seems to be tense, and concentrate on relaxing or letting go in that place. Once that is done, put your mind on the breath again, and inhale and exhale normally while repeating the number *one,* or another one-word mantra, on each exhalation. Begin with five minutes of breath monitoring, gradually working up to twenty minutes per session, if possible, for maximum relaxation response. When you reach your desired time limit, gradually open your eyes and sit quietly, not moving, for a minute or two, then slowly move your arms and feet, finally rising slowly to stand. I find twenty minutes of breath monitoring to be difficult and usually manage to sit for about fifteen minutes. It really doesn't matter, so don't be judgmental if the twenty-minute length is not achieved. Even five minutes will be helpful and can be done several times a day, if necessary.

This exercise calms the mind, relaxes the body, and releases tension in places that other kinds of techniques do not. It is most useful if done on a regular basis, becoming part of a daily routine. Two caveats: first, this exercise should not be done within two hours of eating a big meal since the digestive system is very active then, making it harder for the body to get benefits from the exercise. Second, I have found that doing this exercise within a few hours before a performance makes my body too passive for such an energetic venture. So, if I do it on a day when there will be an evening performance, I do it in the morning and never after lunch. But others may react differently to this. Trial and error will help you find just the right time of day and length for this exercise that applies to your situation.

Find enjoyable pastimes. Over the years, I have done master classes for more than thirty universities, several regional National Association of Teachers of Singing conferences, and other singing organizations. Often, there is a question-and-answer period when students in the audience have an opportunity to ask me anything that comes to mind. Mostly, their questions have concerned aspects of vocal technique, practice habits, career planning, or repertoire. But at almost every event, someone has asked me what I like to do in my free time. A very important way to combat the stress and frenzy of the performing life is to develop outside interests that lend perspective and shape to one's overall existence while promoting relaxation. These diversions can materialize as other forms of artistic expression, such as writing poetry or fiction, painting, or dancing. A vacation from the performance world can be enjoyed through hobbies such as gardening, decorating, or cooking. Intellectual pursuits, such as learning a new language or skill, traveling to do research, or taking classes in another professional field, are popular ways to spend satisfying time. Getting involved in community service and doing charity work is another way to connect to people outside your profession, feel that you are making a difference in people's lives, and gain personal fulfillment from the experience. But for many—and I include myself in this category—the most effective and relaxing diversions are spontaneous: spending an afternoon at a local art gallery or museum, walking the dog in the park, playing a sport, haunting a local bookstore, playing scrabble or bridge, perusing a local shopping mall, or gathering with friends for regular lunch dates and a movie. In short, find diversions of all kinds that promote contentment, and make them a regular part of your life.

Laugh a lot. It turns out that laughter really is the best medicine after all. Numerous health benefits can be derived from laughing on a regular basis. Even fake laughter has been shown to lower blood pressure and anxiety levels. Research has revealed that people feel better physically and emotionally when they laugh and use humor to get through painful or stressful situations. The use of humor also creates better communication with others, resulting in stronger, more lasting relationships as part of the human connection. Laughter helps to break the ice in tense situations, get rid of fears, and diminish critical judgments of ourselves and others. Laughter is infectious and improves a person's overall mood. According to Laughter Yoga International, there are more than six thousand laughter clubs in sixty countries around the world. Some businesses in Japan and other countries set aside time during the workday for employees to gather in front of mirrors to laugh to reduce tension and improve the quality of their productivity. Several well-known doctors, such as Patch Adams (who promoted laugh therapy) and Norman Cousins (*The Anatomy of an Illness*), have written books on the healing affects of laughter. In 2009, over four hundred doctors and professional clowns took part in the Third International Congress of Hospital Clowns to present scientific research that showed laughter as a strong medicine for the body and mind and a tremendous antidote to stress. You don't have to be a clown to use humor as therapy. Anybody can do it. It costs us nothing to look on the light side of things, bring humor into a conversation, or laugh at ourselves when something goes awry. It relaxes the whole body when you have a good, hearty laugh. The result is a reduction in anxiety and tension and a boosted immune system with a release of endorphins, the body's natural feel-good chemicals. With all these positive components, it is a technique that every singer should employ when maneuvering through a performance lifestyle. It is a useful means of establishing rapport with an audience, fellow musicians, and others who cross our path. It is a tremendous tool to use as a coping mechanism in harried, stressful times. Since performers have to take their art seriously to succeed, laughter is a wonderful way to provide a much-needed break, take oneself less seriously for awhile, and see the lighter side of life. So, laugh as often as you can, and hang out with fun people who laugh easily at themselves and life's little roadblocks.

* * *

REMINDERS!

- Visualize the life you want to create.
- Prepare and plan for the life you imagine.
- Make a list of short-term and long-range career goals.
- Develop a workable lifestyle that will bring contentment.
- Research your vocal art: its great performers and style characteristics.
- Decide if a dual-career lifestyle is right for you.
- Don't neglect your inner life.
- Develop satisfying social relationships.
- Get rid of negative thought patterns.
- Develop your EQ.
- Develop positive self-talk that does not compare yourself to others.
- Don't live in the past.
- Use journaling as a tool for expression and monitoring of ideas and feelings.
- Learn to disengage from stress with recuperative downtime.
- Find enjoyable diversions that take your mind off performing.
- Laugh away life's struggles as often as you can.

II

Coping with Success

Over the years, I kept a diary of performance travels and concert notes that contained names of people I met, places I sang, what I sang, how I got there, why I went, an assessment of the performance, lines from reviews, and tidbits about strange, funny, or simply weird happenings before, during, or after the performance. I recommend doing this. It is a great way to remember people and places that are likely to fade from the gray cells after a few years of traveling around. Things start to run together after a while if not jotted down when they are fresh in the mind. So, that's what I did. And I am so glad I did, too, because now I can see them as if they happened yesterday and recall the emotion felt while reading about the events.

Once a singer has prepared well and honed skills to the highest level possible, it is difficult to think that something might still stand in the way of a fabulous performance. I discovered early on that the unexpected is something to be expected. Things happen—things that you never considered before, laugh about, cry about, worry about, didn't prepare for, have to circumnavigate, and deal with on a daily basis. Sometimes these unforeseen occurrences are bizarre, appear out of nowhere, and are the subject of hilarious storytelling among friends at a later date. I've lived through a lot of those in my career. I made it through them, and you can, too.

In the performing life, all kinds of issues occur—some serious and some really zany—that detract from the performance itself and the mindset of the performer. When a crisis sets in, coping skills need to kick in as soon as possible for every artist. A whole lot of humor, a good self-image, better-than-average EQ, and a great support system are helpful personal attributes when faced with hurdles such as logistical problems, malfunctioning equipment, illness, concert venue dilemmas, insomnia, food allergies and diet concerns, and the psychology of recording oneself for posterity. You'll see how all of those coping skills and supportive people came into the picture when reading about some of my performance scenarios. In many cases, disaster would have occurred if I had not leaned on one or more of those elements to solve problems that I faced.

This part of the book relies heavily on my travel diary and that of my accompanist Patsy Wade. I often refer to her or to Rosemary Platt, my other accompanist, by first name in some of the diary entries. The entries contain actual accounts of events that took place in my performing career, as told in diary form, to take you to the scene of each crisis, whether small or large, so that you might experience them as I did. There is an introduction that gives information about the issue being dealt with and a lead-in to each diary entry for the scenario of its performance event. This section is here to offer a little personal advice about how to cope with snags in the performing life and provide, in some cases, much-needed laughter in a profession that often begs for it.

EIGHT

Malfunction Junction

Performers have to contend with lots of variables when planning and executing a performance. Wouldn't it be marvelous if things always ran smoothly, with the performer never having to worry about anything and the mind able to concentrate totally on the artistic endeavor about to unfold? In my naïve student days, I assumed that might be possible.

Unfortunately, no matter how carefully one plans, chaos can take over without notice. Learning to push that chaos aside to give a fine performance is often a tremendous challenge. I recall many times in my career when it seemed as if bumper cars were lined up in front of me blocking my way to the stage. Many incidents were so ludicrous at the time that I literally laughed until I cried. At other times, the *truth is stranger than fiction* scenario that occurred might be found in an addictive page-turner.

LEARN TO READ MAPS

Out-of-town travel to rehearsals and engagements is often a necessity for performers. In a perfect world, I would prefer to avoid reality and just say *Beam me up, Scotty* and not have to contend with today's myriad travel hassles.

I have a performer friend who is contemplating buying a GPS for her car. She complains of having to read maps to get to where she's going after being misled several times by incorrect Internet directions. However, having heard horror stories about GPS inaccuracies, she's being held back by fears of ending up in a swamp and missing a performance date, having followed the GPS directions to a destination that doesn't really exist. What to do? I say, learn to read maps, just in case.

When I began my career in the late 1970s, I didn't have to worry about those decisions. Map reading was the gold standard. One of my earliest professional concerts was at Indiana State University, where a large three-day new music festival was being held. About three weeks prior to the event, one of the scheduled singers became ill and canceled. Thus, I was called by one of the organizers, who inquired about my availability to sing one of the featured works, Dominick Argento's Pulitzer Prize–winning song cycle *The Diary of Virginia Woolf*. She had just heard me sing it at the National Association of Teachers of Singing convention in Philadelphia. I jumped at the chance to perform it again, especially when I heard the names of the fine performers already scheduled for the festival.

So, the trip was planned quickly. We would fly. Why I didn't pay attention to the auto route from my house to Terre Haute, Indiana, is a dim memory now. Apparently, it is only a four-and-half-hour drive. Perhaps I feared it would snow, who knows? But . . .

* * *

Dear Diary,
    March . . . home of host, 10:30 pm , night before performance . . . Terre Haute
    Louisville's airport, surprisingly modern. Cincinnati's and Nashville's really need work.

Terre Haute's? Got here too late in the evening to make a judgment, all closed up and vacant. Never expected to see all four on this trip.

Plane left Nashville two hours late, missed connection in Louisville, waited in Tiki-style restaurant, eating something Hawaiian, drinking a mai tai—mostly fruit juice, we thought—while they tried to rebook us.

Heard my name over intercom, lurched out of the booth, paid, started up the ramp to ticket area. Where is Patsy?

Looked back. Patsy standing about twenty yards behind holding onto rail looking shorter than her usual 5'1". Uh oh, she had two mai tai's. Ran back in her direction. "Where are we going?" she said in a small, odd, scratchy voice as I pulled her down the hall to the ticket counter.

No luck. No plane tonight. Had to stay in Louisville. Motel near airport. Small, too hot, cramped, prison lighting, not much sleep. Doors banging and people talking in the hall all night.

Up early for plane to Terre Haute. "Not today," said the smiling stewardess. Plane had a malfunction. Instead, booked to Cincinnati. How nice, never been there. Isn't that the wrong direction?

Arrived on time, rushed to meet connection to Terre Haute.

Called our Terre Haute host for third time. "We're finally on our way," I told her.

Took off on time. Celebration!!

Not so fast!

Would have arrived in time for our on-stage rehearsal at 8:00 pm if the two pilots on the tiny four-passenger plane had not gotten lost.

Have made a resolution. Never again fly on a plane where I can see pilots searching maps and hear them calling the airport to find out where they are while flying through thick clouds and pelting rain with no land in sight. I like to be unaware that we are forty miles off course and headed in the wrong direction.

Had to turn back, making us arrive an hour and a half late.

Will have to perform cold. Wonder what that stage looks like? Will I be able to hear myself?

So much for leaving a day early to be rested and make the rehearsal schedule.

Trying not to obsess. Patsy worried about the piano. What kind is it? Do the pedals work?

Surely!

Dead tired, got to get to sleep, not sleepy, can hardly see to read.

Two days, four airports, three planes, each smaller than the one before. There must be a faster way to get here.

* * *

Later . . . after concert

Fabulous concert! Superb performers.

Beautiful hall. Good acoustics.

Full house. Well-received. No problems. Relief!

We're happy! We can do this! Went better than Philadelphia.

Heard *Ancient Voices of Children* (Crumb) live for first time. Impressive performance by Elizabeth Mannion. Wow, what a piece!!! Have to sing that!

On to the next!

* * *

BEWARE OF ALLEYS

In 1988, I was fortunate to receive a National Endowment for the Arts Solo Recitalist Grant to sing programs of American art song in St. Louis, Boston, and Washington, DC. The second in this series was in Boston at the Longy School of Music with an additional performance and interview scheduled for the day before the concert on the much-lauded WGBH radio program *Chamber Works*.

I have always been an obsessive planner, double-checking plane flights, hotel accommodations, and other concert details. This occasion was no different. However, Murphy's law kicked in just about the time I arrived at the Nashville airport for our 9:30 am flight to Boston. Patsy met me there to find out that the plane was delayed and we'd be leaving in about two hours. Since it was a direct flight, we didn't worry. We would still arrive in Boston by midafternoon, plenty of time to eat and rest for the next two days of concerts. But . . .

* * *

Dear Diary,
    October . . . 1:00 am . . . Copley Plaza Hotel (sort of), Boston
    Surprise! Rescheduled flight to Boston through Washington got here early, according to the giddy-sounding pilot. Arrived at 11:30 pm.
    Beautiful hotel, the Copley Plaza. Gleaming marble, wood and brass lobby, mountainous floral arrangements.
    Tall night manager, smiling, has news; our reservation was cancelled, given away due to some overflow event. But I had confirmed late arrival!
    No good explanation. Were we the only ones bumped?
    Worn-out from long day, airports, not enough protein, I stared as Patsy talked faster and faster—we have to perform tomorrow and the next day, something about radios and concert halls. I tried to focus on her lips but they were a blur.
    "I've found another place to put you for the night," he said finally, whisking a key from under the counter. "Come back to the desk tomorrow morning after breakfast for your regular room."
    Off we went! Was the substitute hotel nearby?
    The huge chandelier was sparkling as we followed him through the lobby, down a long hall, out the back door, through an alley, and stopped at what must have been the door to a speakeasy in another era. Do we need a password?
    Once inside, we stare. Ahead is long hall with lots of small doors. Odd, but familiar.
    I saw this movie. I think it was *One Flew over the Cuckoo's Nest*.
    Bare-bulb hallway lighting. One door opens, Patsy goes in. Second door opens, I go in.
    Couldn't stay together, rooms not big enough.
    Barracks is not the right word for this room. *Cubicle*, perhaps *cell*. Even dorm rooms have windows.
    No phone, no pictures, no TV, one small bed with pale beige cover and flat pillow.
    Ow! Bathroom too small to brush teeth without hitting wall with elbow.
    Why does that light keep flickering?
    Think on the positive side. It *looks* clean.

* * *

Later . . . last night in Boston
   Love this city!!
   Survived camp Copley. Repentant after all.
   Second and third nights, very large, beautiful suite, huge welcome basket of fruit, and vases of fresh flowers.
   Loved those big breakfasts, incredible pastries with marzipan topping.
   Live radio show a blast. Good karma with host, who kept talking about the Rhian Samuel pieces. He'd never heard her music!
   Oh, my, the Ives song. What were those words I sang? Mics in your face do funny things to the brain.
   Longy concert smooth as silk, fun. Friendly audience liked American music. Enjoyed after concert food/chat with composer Laura Clayton—sang one of her pieces (*Herself the Tide*)—and husband/artist Paul Pollaro. A rare treat!

* * *

CHECK EQUIPMENT TWICE

I have always loved to sing weird, experimental music with unusual accompaniments and extravagant vocal techniques. In my early career, many of my performances involved electronic equipment: microphones, special lighting, tape players, and so on, because in those days, it was all the rage. Composers were writing a lot of that kind of music, and not many singers were willing to give it a try. So, I made my mark.
   In the 1970s and 1980s, I sang several fascinating compositions that were written for voice and prerecorded four-channel tape that required special equipment for accurate playback during the concert. The equipment was not always available, and finding a qualified person on site to set it up and run it was even harder. So, I programmed that kind of contemporary music only at my university or on out-of-town concerts when I was assured that the equipment and personnel were in place. However, the unexpected can happen, and in the face of disaster, you just have to forge onward.
   For instance . . .

* * *

Dear Diary,
   December . . . Louisville . . . night before performance, National NATS Convention
   Arrived a day early to rehearse for concert tomorrow morning at 10:00.

Dead, carpeted hotel ballroom. No surprise there. Usual for conventions.

Great rehearsal with Patsy for Kenton Coe pieces (*London Songs*) and technical crew for Ramon Zupko electronic piece (*Voices*). Mesmerizing, exciting work! Can't wait for crowd reaction.

Limited time in hall. Only got one run-through with electronics.

Surprised, no problems with equipment. Should be fine. Can sleep easy tonight.

* * *

Later . . . after concert, the best laid plans, etc. . .

Up early. Vocal warm-ups in hotel bathroom. Wish the concert hall was this live.

Arrived concert hall, 9:30 am. Engineer madly plugging and unplugging equipment.

Everything OK? Thumbs up!

Showtime! Overflow crowd. Coe pieces first. Enthusiastic applause.

Talked to audience about Zupko—listen for strange, taped sounds, unfamiliar vocal techniques.

Expectant faces, waiting.

Lights dim. Tape sounds emit eerily.

What was that? Sounds odd. Not a good odd!

Concentrate. Start singing.

Strange noises, not Zupko's noises. New noises.

Don't remember any buzzes. Did he revise it overnight? Thought he was in Michigan. Glad he's in Michigan!

Keep singing.

Something missing. Where's the surround sound?

Where's my entrance? Tape cues gone.

Can't hear the taped voices. Ah! Only two channels playing.

Just keep singing!

Thank God, it's over! Applause, applause.

Smiles. New music fans rush forward.

"Congratulations!" "Interesting piece." "Never heard anything like it!"

Favorite comment: "Wow, loved those buzzes. Wanna hear that again!"

* * *

IGNORE THE DISSONANCE

By midcareer, I had become known for singing music by women composers, one of my passions. Among a long list of guest artist recitals for which I was engaged was one at Rhodes College in Memphis, Tennessee. This concert was devoted to music of Lili Boulanger, Rhian Samuel, Elizabeth Vercoe, Mary Howe, and other women. Some of it, like the Boulanger, was quite melodic, but other pieces sounded more contemporary with unusual vocal techniques and angular melody lines, not ones you can whistle. The lovely, acoustically perfect auditorium was filled as Patsy and I walked onto the stage. Then . . .

* * *

Dear Diary,

September . . . Memphis . . . day after concert . . . Rhodes College

Headed home. Reliving concert. Laughing.

Enthusiastic audience. Great response to music. Sang two encores. Wonderful people. Lots of fun!

Patsy driving. Laughing, crying, reminiscing.

What was that thin high-pitched tone during first Boulanger piece?

Thought it was air conditioning system. Seemed to hover just a half step above every note I held at phrase ends.

Boulanger, dissonant?

Second Boulanger piece—pin-pointed origin of tone. Coming from audience left side, getting louder.

I thought this was a solo, not a duet.

Don't look! Make bigger crescendos.

Patsy driving, laughing, mascara running. I'm recalling.

What a creative tone, moved up and down in pitch at will, always just a shade off from one I'm singing.

Improvisation. Wow!

Audience heads turn, searching to recognize guest composer of tones.

Third Boulanger, a three page song.

Two pages, I'm all alone. No spine tingling, knife scraping sounds. Where did it go?

One page to go. Hurry! Fast approaching high note on last line.

Almost there, going to make it!

Darn, it got there first. Settled in just under my pitch, a nice minor second. Eye-crossing!

Sang last note. Applause. Walk faster. Giggle starting to bubble up.

Dare not look at Patsy until offstage.

Tone still pinging off ceiling moving up a major third.

All laughed out, I pull out the terrific review in today's Memphis Commercial Appeal.

Read it to Patsy. Get to part where reviewer says, "The women were unfazed . . . and didn't even fold their hands when a hearing aid inadvertently squealed during three pieces."

Have to stop. Patsy can't see to drive.

Laughing, crying, laughing!

NINE

I Can't Eat That!

Singers have to be careful about what they eat right before a performance. Certain foods, like sugary snacks and drinks, chocolate, or milk
products, can goo up the throat and make the voice sound like it is trying
desperately to get through a very thick curtain of gauze. Sometimes,
foods that most people enjoy without regret can bring about dramatic
voice changes in singers who are sensitive to them. I've taught several
singers who discovered odd allergies or sensitivities to corn, wine, wheat,
citrus fruits, and spices that made their voices hoarse, breathy, or crackly
and unable to sustain a pitch evenly. It was perplexing, since the vocal
cords showed no sign of a problem when viewed by a laryngologist. Each
had to go through allergy testing and food elimination diets to figure out
that they needed to avoid certain items. In all cases, the problem was
eventually solved when the culprit was discovered.

Early in the 1980s, I'd had suspicions—for a short while—that milk
products were affecting my digestion negatively, but it became perfectly
clear that they were also affecting my voice negatively when I went to
Columbus, Ohio, to make a recording, *Music by Women Composers*, with
Rosemary Platt. I had traveled there to record the pieces in her acoustically perfect auditorium at Ohio State University. We spent three days lay-
ing down the tracks. It was tiring work, and we were a bit worn out by
the end of the process. Being pleased with the results so far, we decided
to celebrate after the last full recording session. We were scheduled to
meet with the engineer the following day to take a final listen to see if any
bit, large or small, needed to be redone, but we craved—and deserved—a
break. She suggested her favorite ice cream parlor, which was famous for
concocting all kinds of delicacies. I indulged in a luscious, large banana
split with three different kinds of ice cream and lots of trimmings. I
hadn't eaten that much of any kind of milk product in one sitting in

125

years. By the time I finished it off, I realized that my speaking voice was disappearing. I could hardly talk. It was getting feathery and felt scratchy, but it didn't occur to me that my singing voice might still be dramatically affected the next day. When I woke up the next morning, I had little voice with which to sing. The tone was breathy and just wouldn't focus in a normal way. I spent a good while warming it up very slowly, trying to coax it into action, in case I would need to redo any short sections once we listened to the final cuts. It eventually improved a little but not to the point where I would have been secure in recording anything. Fortunately, we were pleased with all of the songs we heard that morning and felt that nothing had to be recorded again. I got lucky in this case and learned my lesson. From that day forward, I never ate or drank milk products within days of a performance date and eventually had to give them up altogether to improve my overall health.

Some singers eat too much, too fast, or too near the time of a concert, or they choose overly acidic, spicy, or sugary foods and carbonated or caffeinated drinks, any of which can cause problems with breathing, burping, reflux, heartburn, or general lethargy. Sometimes, a concert venue will provide tables of drinks and food backstage for the performers. It is tempting to partake; after all, it's free food and looks good. But that could be disastrous if you are not familiar with a particular food choice and its seasoning or if the food is of the wrong kind and will not promote vocal clarity or might deplete your energy and cause digestive upsets. A venue's thoughtfulness could be a singer's downfall. So, singers have to be careful what they eat and drink backstage before and during a concert.

I remember a concert tour to England when a venue provided a large pitcher of a drink they call "squash." I learned later that it is generally made of a concentrated syrup of fruit juices, sugar, and water, sometimes herbal extracts, and is usually very fizzy. It looked luscious, but I had never had that drink before and wasn't sure if I should imbibe just before going onto the stage. My accompanist tasted it for me and said it was very acidic and might likely irritate my throat. I passed on it.

There are occasions, especially when on the road for concerts, when a singer's food requirements are difficult to manage due to tight schedules, the availability of acceptable food choices, and unforeseen problems with the food preparation. I recall quite a few times when the lack of appropriate choices, secret and unexpected ingredients, or labeling mistakes have caused more than a little concern right before, during, or after a performance.

Sometimes people put things in packages that they do not belong in. I learned that lesson on a trip to sing a recital and do master classes at Delta State University in Mississippi. Patsy and I were housed in extremely comfortable guest accommodations, with two bedrooms, a kitchen, and living room and all the amenities one could want, including snacks, tea, and coffee—the coffee tin said *decaf.* I rarely drink coffee, and

I always drink decaf when I do, but we decided to indulge in a cup of hot coffee and a snack when we got back to our lodgings after a successful concert. The coffee was so good that we each had two cups; after all, it was decaf. It was fortunate that we waited until after the concert for this adventure, since what we thought was decaf was obviously not. Around midnight, we realized that both of us felt really hyper. I think I could have run a 5K. We never slept a wink all night long, up talking and walking around until time to leave for home the next morning. We drove home the next day still feeling jittery from all of the caffeine. So, timing of meals and food selection are important factors to take seriously right before a performance or when you require much-needed sleep.

ASK THE WAITER TWICE

I love to try new foods but have learned that the days leading up to a performance are not the time to be adventurous. So, I never do that on purpose. My performance-day meals of choice are rather bland: lean protein, a plain baked potato, and vegetables with a little salt and no other spices, especially pepper, which tends to make me cough—not a good thing for a singer. I can manage that kind of meal easily when I'm at home. But when on the road for an engagement and having to eat every meal in a restaurant, it isn't always easy to find such plain food. I've discovered that even when waiters are quizzed about how something is prepared, you can never be absolutely certain of exactly what will end up in your stomach. There was one vivid occasion when I was in Winchester, Virginia, for a few days to do a recital and master classes for Shenandoah Conservatory. Everything had been beautifully arranged for our stay until . . .

* * *

Dear Diary,
October . . . hotel room . . . night before recital . . . Shenandoah Conservatory
Lovely place. Gorgeous scenery. Most congenial host.
Delightful master classes. Marvelous singers!
Hosted for dinner by faculty at lovely dark-paneled, historic restaurant.
Good conversation, friendly folks!
Strange-sounding menu selections. Have to be careful.
Wait! Tuna steak, rice and steamed vegetables seems OK.
Quiz waiter. "Plain, but delicious. Just a little salt," he says.
Fabulous!
Tuna arrives. Good. Odd flavor. Just salt? Probably imagining it.
8:30. Back at hotel. Getting undressed. Suddenly feel hot.
Air conditioning working? Walk past Patsy to check it out.
"Have you looked in the mirror?" she asks.

Bright red is usually my color. Not this time.

Blotches, middle of chest, up neck, onto face. Panic.

"You're not having trouble breathing, are you?"

Throat feels itchy. Cold cloths, ice water, constant checking in the mirror.

Call a doctor? No, not yet, might give me something that would make it worse.

Take allergy pill.

11:00 pm. Skin now a lighter shade of red. Lip puffy.

Read, watch TV, mind still on lobster skin.

More cold cloths.

Lights out, take sleeping pill. Dream about tuna.

* * *

Next day . . . after recital . . .

Woke early. Rested all day.

Worried. Throat still scratchy. No talking.

Slow vocal warm-up. Throat Coat Tea and Hall's.

Put on makeup with spatula. Good diversion.

Showtime! Relief! Voice fine. Good concert, considering. Never mentioned allergy.

Lobster skin diminished. Small blotches on neck, one over right eye, slightly swollen lip.

Matched red sequined dress beautifully.

* * *

HAVE A PROGRESSIVE DINNER

One of my favorite memories—one that makes me laugh as I write this—involves a road trip to Arkansas back in the 1990s. I was invited to do a master class and sing a recital for several hundred singers from college age to preprofessional level at a regional National Association of Teachers of Singing convention that was held at two universities, across the street from each other, in the same town. Patsy and I had a lovely drive there, enjoyed lunch in a beautiful tearoom in the middle of town, and checked into our hotel. Though we made contact with a local host when we went to the university to check out the concert hall, no information was exchanged about a good place to eat dinner before our concert that evening. However, our motel, being on the outskirts of town, was in a busy area that displayed a few restaurant signs and possibilities. After getting a recommendation from the desk clerk, we set out for an early dinner only to find . . .

* * *

Dear Diary,

Motel room . . . before concert

Starving!!! Didn't have enough dinner.

Went to desk clerk's favorite place, looked at menu, got back into car. Even the menu looked fried.

Starving, starving!!!

Two blocks down found a homey-looking place with buffet. Promising.

Hold on. No good choices. Only meat was fried chicken and polish sausage.

Chose chicken. Peeled off crispy skin, sole-leather meat inedible.

Rubbery green beans refused to get on fork.

Everything else the same color, white. Nope, can't do this.

Napkins folded, Patsy headed for the door as I paid.

Got to find something to eat. Concert hour looming.

"Let's try that." Patsy pointed across the road as my car lurched over a huge dip and around the McDonald's drive-through.

Can't believe I'm going to sing a concert having eaten a McDonald's hamburger (without cheese, of course).

* * *

Later . . . after concert . . . searching for vending machine

Huge crowd. Very large hall, multipurpose.

Poor acoustics. Should have used mic as host suggested.

Concert had flow. Felt good. Mobbed by singers. Autographed programs 'til hand cramped up.

Starving, starving, starving!!! Got to find some crackers.

* * *

WHERE'S THE BEEF?

I have lived in the South all of my life, and I grew up eating hearty meals but generally healthful ones filled with fresh vegetables, baked and roasted meats, with a little fried chicken and shrimp thrown in, followed by lots of homemade desserts. I gave up the desserts and the "bad for you" stuff thirty years ago. I limit sugar, don't eat processed foods, and haven't had a carbonated soda since 1965, when a friend showed me how to get a dead, corroded car battery started again by pouring a Pepsi over it. Since I don't eat milk products, there are no scoops of ice cream, wedges of cheese, dollops of sour cream, or mounds of butter in my diet. However, I told my doctor that I won't give up my two slices of bacon in the morning no matter what happens. Though I'm only 5'3" and around 120 pounds, I still require three square meals a day with plenty of protein, whole grain bread, colorful vegetables, and fruit. As one concert host put it, "you sure do eat a lot for a little thing." I guess so, but I can't live without it and certainly can't sing without a good bit of sustenance.

I love the flavor of food and enjoy different textures. So, it is no accident that I've planned whole vacations around restaurant choices. However, I've come to realize that there is a world of people out there who hate food, are constantly on some strange deprivation diet, have weak taste buds and happily eat anything bland, or live in perpetual fear of eating something that might kill them before their time. They live on what my aunt, a fabulous country cook, would have called, "rabbit food." I must say that I don't know any singers in this category, though I'm sure they exist. Most of the singers I know eat well and often and gear their meals toward the support of the large amount of energy required to sustain their bodies and voices through performances and rehearsals. That doesn't mean they eat unhealthily, just heartily.

During my travels, I've connected with a few hosts whose eating habits were wildly different from my own. But being aware that I might need to have food that they found disgusting, they went overboard to see that I was able to get access to it. However, there were a couple of hosts who seemed oblivious to any diet but their own and appeared dedicated to proselytism. I recall a four-day period when my accompanist and I traveled to a major metropolitan area to perform two concerts, do radio interviews, and rehearse a new work that we would premiere. We had a generous, gregarious host who provided us with comfortable accommodations and drove us everywhere we needed to go. She was not a musician, but she was a great supporter of the arts. It turned out that . . .

* * *

Dear Diary,
   Day two . . . sneaking into host's kitchen . . . 4:00 pm.
   Tiptoeing down the hall, we remembered she had said, "Make yourselves at home."
   Wow, what a kitchen! Where to start looking?
   Cupboard doors opened and closed.
   Nothing but salt-free crackers, a loaf of spelt and some kind of wafers that looked like Styrofoam. Two bins of flax seeds.
   Groan.
   "I don't have enough energy to lift my fingers onto the keyboard tonight, much less play that Rochberg."
   "I know, I've got to find some protein or my high notes are goners."
   "Maybe dinner will have some meat in it this time."
   "Not unless it crawls on the plate while she's not looking."

"Surely there's something in the fridge."

Why are we whispering? She's gone.

Two heads stare into the bright light of the glass shelves.

Tupperware bins filled with tofu, cottage cheese, every known kind of lettuce and herb.

One whole crisper stuffed with carrots and celery.

"My skin is going to turn orange before tomorrow and I just hate the texture of raw celery."

"I refuse to drink another basil and lettuce smoothie. That stuff was foul."

"I've hinted about the meat, but no takers. She's a dyed-in-the-wool micro-portion vegetarian."

"Well, tomorrow we're buying some lunch meat."

"OK. Wait, what's that in the back of that shelf?"

"Hallelujah. I'll grab that bread we saw over there."

Peanut butter and spelt make a pretty good sandwich.

* * *

Day four . . . in taxi on the way to airport

"If I ever see another mock beefburger made out of tofu, I'll have to call 911."

"I just couldn't eat that, but she didn't seem to mind that I took it back to the kitchen and came out with something else."

"Thank goodness we bought that two pounds of lunchmeat and the potato salad. That's the only thing that saved dinner."

"Well, at least it gave me enough energy to get through the concert."

"I'm sure she threw the rest of it out before our taxi left her driveway."

"Oh, I ate the rest of that last night in my room after she went to bed."

"Poor woman went pale when I ordered that lasagna at the restaurant after the concert. I just had to have some beef."

"Here's the airport."

"Thank God. Let's head to the restaurant as soon we check in. I've got to have some additives."

TEN

Sleep Is Not a Perk

Singers have to have sleep. Some need sleep more than others, but for the body and voice to be in peak performance mode, sleep is essential. It is said that Thomas Edison, the inventor, slept only three or four hours a night, and Jay Leno says that he does just fine with five. I can't imagine existing on that little sleep. I would become a permanent zombie.

I am at my best for singing, teaching, or just daily living when I've had eight hours of uninterrupted sleep in a quiet dark room with my little sound machine making wind or water noises and the room temperature at about sixty-five degrees. Unfortunately, that ideal condition couldn't always be duplicated when I was traveling to sing concerts, causing unwanted stress and fatigue, especially in the early years.

"Are we ever going to sleep?" asked Rosemary Platt, rising up from her bed in an Atlanta motel room just as the big hand reached midnight Eastern time. I thought she was asleep. The television was almost inaudible but spilling light from the Johnny Carson show into the otherwise darkened room. I was wide awake with no sleep in sight. Poor Rosemary. This trip took place back in the mid-1980s when we were invited to perform at the International Congress on Women in Music. It was the first time that we traveled together and the only time we stayed in the same room. I apologized profusely, turned off the TV so that she could go to sleep, and lay awake for another three hours, waiting for the four thousandth sheep to jump over that fence.

Many people have no trouble falling asleep and can do it almost anywhere, no matter the noise around them, how many bright lights are on in the room, or what time of day it is. They do not know what a gift it is to be able to slumber at will. I am constantly amazed at my husband of forty-four years, who will occasionally announce something like this: "I have to get up at 5:30 in the morning to leave for the airport, so I'm going to sleep at 8:30 tonight." He will go off to bed at 8:30, and ten minutes later will be fast asleep. I have no empathy with that kind of person.

I've never been a good sleeper. My body has never wanted to go to bed before midnight, and I wake up at the slightest noise. So, when I was a child, being forced to go to bed at 9:00 with lights out was akin to mental torture. I remember lying awake in my bed and waiting for my parents to go to their room. Then, I'd creep down the hall to the kitchen to get a snack, turn on the small bedside light in my room, and read a story. As a teenager, I'd sneak into the living room and watch TV when there was finally something on it other than the test pattern after 10:00 pm—these were the olden days, for those who don't know what a test pattern is. As an only child, I slept in a room away from noise at home and never had sleepovers at a friend's house. So, I was used to quiet, solitude, and having the whole room to myself. When we traveled on vacation, which was rare, I always had trouble sleeping in a strange place. This difficulty falling asleep became even more pronounced when I went away to college and suddenly had a roommate. But I eventually became accustomed to it, and my sleep patterns evened out with no dramatic problems for several years.

Unfortunately, things did not stay in that good place. Somewhere in my early thirties, the "can't get to sleep" demon raised its head again and became a real issue when traveling for concerts or when I was at home and involved in late-night rehearsals. The first and most dramatic time that I recall insomnia being a real issue was back in the early 1980s when my university's opera theatre staged a production of Sondheim's *A Little Night Music* in which I played Desiree Armfeldt. I was teaching during the day and rehearsing every night for the two weeks prior to the performances. During that period of nightly rehearsals that ended at 10:30 pm, I found it increasingly difficult and eventually impossible to go to sleep. My mind and body would get so revved up by the rehearsal that it took several hours to come down into a calm, quiet state where sleep could happen; sometimes, that would not be until four or five in the morning, almost time to get up to go and teach. On three nights, I did not sleep at all. Nothing I tried seemed to help, which made me even more anxious about getting some sleep. My doctor's solutions were to sleep in a room by myself, take a prescription muscle relaxer, drink chamomile tea, and change my teaching schedule slightly. His suggestions helped somewhat, but it was a struggle to make it through the production. I was burning the candle at both ends. Though I made it through successfully without any vocal or memory problems, it definitely took a toll on my physical strength. It was several weeks before I recovered from that onslaught of insomnia and felt like myself again.

As I began to travel more for singing engagements, there were other things that negatively affected my ability to go to sleep. First, changing time zones on concert trips was problematic, especially when I went several time zones beyond my own. I recall a trip to Fairbanks, Alaska, to sing at an international music festival when I had to cross three time zones. Plus, the sun didn't set there until almost 11:00 pm. That was particularly difficult. My body simply didn't know when to go to sleep for the five days I was there.

Another situation that grew more difficult when traveling was sleeping in the room with someone else. Strangely, sleeplessness was made competitive when sharing a room with someone who was asleep and enjoying it, especially if that person was snoring. There is something quite irritating about watching someone sleep when you can't seem to do it. My anxiety about not going to sleep tended to increase, knowing that I needed to sleep to be in good voice and optimum energy for the performance the next day. So, it was best not to share a room with anyone, to be free of sleep competition.

I didn't have any good tools to deal with this problem for several years, though I took advice from doctors, read everything I could find on sleep problems, tried a couple of over-the-counter and prescription sleeping pills—I am not a happy pill taker and resist them at all costs—and all kinds of herbal remedies, relaxation techniques, and other suggestions. Nothing really worked well on a regular basis. Sometimes I was able to sleep just fine, and sometimes it was agony. I suspect a combination of several things contributed to sleep distress, but strange surroundings, a built-up anticipation of travel insomnia, the excitement of an upcoming performance, a change in my normal schedule, and a simmering generalized anxiety that seems to be inherent in some members of my family were primary issues.

I am not the only one who has experienced this problem. In fact, it is quite common. Everyone has a sleepless night now and again. But for performers who feel pressure to be at their best when it's time to go onstage, those sleepless nights that turn into chronic insomnia can become quite stressful. Several of my former students who are now performers have called me to ask advice in trying to tackle this issue. I've performed with professional singers who told me that their ability to sleep had been compromised by one thing or another and were having difficulty coping and suffering from fatigue. It is essential that every singer who has this problem seek professional advice from a family physician, a sleep specialist, or perhaps a counselor to find ways to combat it. Otherwise, it will probably not go away by itself and may pose difficulties in developing a long-term career in performance.

About twenty years ago, I finally found some workable answers for my problem that changed the course of traveling to do concerts and made sleeping less of an issue, though I still don't want to go to bed before midnight. My routine today involves several things that help set my mind and body into the proper restful mood for achieving a good night's sleep. I turn off all the lights in my room, making it as dark as possible, at least an hour before I want to fall asleep. I do not eat or drink anything that contains caffeine for two or three days before a concert performance. I avoid foods that are known to cause digestive upsets. I try to get a little exercise from walking or tai chi early in the day. I use the four–seven–eight breathing technique I mention earlier in this book (see chapter 7) and repeat it several times a day starting three days before the performance. I take my travel-size sleep machine with me on all trips. It can be set at different volume levels and sound choices, from white noise to pleasant rippling brooks or wind whistling through trees: continuous sounds that lull me to sleep. I use a soothing mantra that I repeat silently on each breath—such as *peace, quiet, harmony*—for about ten minutes after getting comfortable in my bed. Sometimes that alone will allow my mind to relax and fall asleep within minutes. Finally, I take my prescription sleeping medication with me to use as a last resort. I use a very small amount when everything else has failed. It has been a lifesaver and changed the course of my performing career, as you will soon read. I'm certain that if I had not found these solutions, I would have chosen to curtail performing, except in local venues, due to the stress and fatigue caused by insomnia during periods of late rehearsals and nights on the road right before a concert.

WHAT TIME IS IT?

By the late 1980s, there had been several times when I had trouble sleeping while on tour for concerts. Somehow, I had managed to cope in all cases with very little sleep the night before the concert. A perfect example was during a recital tour made possible by a grant from the National Endowment for the Arts Recitalist Fellowship. Patsy and I were in St. Louis, Missouri, to perform a concert at the magnificent Sheldon Concert Hall, recognized as one of the nation's finest performing facilities. Everything went like clockwork; we arrived a day early without incident, had an excellent rehearsal in the hall—perfect acoustics—checked into the hotel, enjoyed a lovely dinner at a local restaurant, and settled into our room for a night of relaxation after a long drive and rehearsal, anticipating a good night's sleep when . . .

* * *

Dear Diary,
   September . . . St. Louis . . . hotel room . . . night before concert
   TV blares through Tonight Show. Patsy not sleepy, I'm not sleepy.
   Turn off lights, maybe that will help. Turn down TV to mumble level.
   Decide to watch rerun of *Happy Days*.
   Patsy quiet now, drifted off, turned over in her bed. I'm not sleepy.

Large clock next to my right ear says 1:00 am. Got to get some sleep.

Turn off TV. Darkness. Not exactly, flashing neon light shining through curtain sliver. Won't close to block it out. Safety pin didn't work.

Wait for sleep.

Allow mind to become blank. No thinking. Wait.

No sleep in sight.

Startled by air-conditioning unit's abrupt trigger. Slams on, then off, every five minutes.

Clock ticking, ticking, ticking. Oh no!

Tried to lift it. Ugh! Bolted to nightstand. Can't turn it off. Lighted dial shouts 2:00 am.

Go to bathroom, get small towel, cover clock. Now, gagged ticking.

Search quietly through suitcase. Find Agatha Christie.

Should have brought nightlight for reading. Bedside lamp will disturb Patsy.

Slink toward bathroom with desk chair. Whack. Chair won't go through door.

Patsy still sleeping. Thank goodness.

Sitting on toilet lid reading chapter twelve. Watch says 3:30.

Bright bathroom lights. Shower curtain has exactly 23 etched frogs on it. One's missing a leg.

No sleep in sight. Can hear faint tick, tick, tick from other room.

* * *

Hotel room . . . after concert

Felt really good about the concert. Beautiful, spacious hall.

In good voice. Great response from audience.

Lovely reception at home of local singer.

Can't believe I had to sing with only two hours' sleep.

Tried to nap before concert, no luck. Not a napper.

Had to will my way through this one.

Not fun until on the stage, then clear sailing.

Got to solve this sleeping problem and pack a hammer for the next road trip.

* * *

CALL FOR HELP

In June 1995, I was scheduled to sing a recital on the regular season concert series of the National Gallery of Art in Washington, DC. The concert was to be broadcast on National Public Radio, and the venue representative expected there to be a capacity crowd in the hall. It was a very exciting venture, one that I had been looking forward to for several months. This would be the first time I had performed in a major venue in almost a year, having been ill, then taken a few months off to fully recover from major surgery before launching into the performance mode once again. I had been cleared to sing by my doctors. I felt energetic; my voice was in good shape; and I had plenty of time to prepare the music for the concert. Plus, Patsy and I had tried out the recital in two regional venues so that it would be polished for this high-pressure event. So, I was in a very good place, vocally, mentally, and physically when we boarded the plane for Washington. Patsy, my husband George, and I arrived in the late afternoon the day before the concert and had a pleasant early-evening dinner in a lovely restaurant that had been recommended by a local gourmand. We were anticipating a rehearsal in the performance space the next morning at 11:00—the day of the concert. It was a jolly evening filled with expectation.

Back at the hotel, Patsy went to her room and we to ours around 9:00. Then . . .

* * *

Dear Diary,
Washington hotel room . . . night before concert
It's amazing how a person can go to sleep just by saying, "I'm going to sleep now."

That was at 9:30. Even the TV doesn't bother him. How annoying!!

Walk out into hall and down to the lobby. Got to get out of the room for a while. Feel trapped in small space. Already worried about not sleeping.

Back to the room for a few breathing exercises. Relax!

Midnight. Eyes wide open. Revved-up. Could easily do a hundred push-ups.

All lights off. TV quietly emitting late-night talk show.

1:00 am. "Are you still awake?" he asks, getting up to drink water.

Lies back down, falls asleep immediately. How does he do that?

Scanning through channels, reruns and old movies.

1:45 am. He sits up in bed. "You'd better go to sleep or you'll never make that rehearsal."

"Sorry, I just can't sleep on demand."

He immediately falls back to sleep. Soft snoring.

Turn TV off, grab mindless novel and reading light.

Reading, reading, reading, reading, Reading, READING!

2:30 am. Time to eat crackers. Still not sleepy.

"Oh, sleep why dost thou leave me?" Hate Handel. Not singing that tomorrow.

Gurgles drift from left side of bed.

My dear doctor, who knows my history of medical emergencies and allergies to drugs, had said, "Call me at home if you get anxious or have a problem on the road. I'm always here if you need me."

Did she really mean that? Should I call her? Never done that before.

Start searching address book for doctor's home phone number.

3:00 am. Eastern Time (2:00 am body time). No sleep in my future. Turn on bedside light.

George still asleep. Softly snoring. Unbelievable. Where's my whistle?

Pick up phone and dial Nashville number. Three rings and "Hello?"

"I'm so sorry to call you at 2:00 in the morning but" . . . explain details.

George, finally awake, mouths, "Who is that?"

Doctor so sorry she forgot to give me prescription for sleeping pills.

She asks, "Is there an all-night pharmacy nearby?"

How would I know? This is Washington, DC.

Have to check with desk clerk. Will call her back.

"Can George go and pick it up if I call it in?" George, Mr. World's-Best Support System, already putting on pants.

Desk clerk provides nearby pharmacy phone number. Call back doctor, who calls it in.

Assures me it will work, not to worry. I'll sleep like a baby and be just fine.

Won't bother my voice.

George goes downstairs to get cab to pharmacy while I wait.

Start to feel relieved. He'll be back soon and I'll be asleep.

* * *

After concert . . . celebrating . . . reliving last 24 hours

George describes trip to pharmacy; a sitcom complete with laugh track.

Bellhop whistles for cab at 3:45 am. Gives cabbie instructions, warns him to take direct route to CVS pharmacy address. No sightseeing. Cabbie agrees.

"It's only a few minutes away," says bellhop. Off they go.

Dark streets, nice neighborhoods change to low-rent, slum businesses, bars, neon signs, nightclubs. Cabbie gives travelogue.

George wonders. Is this the right way? Will I be mugged?

Red-light district. Hold on. What's that over there?

Cabbie preaches hell-fire and damnation against passing women of the night and low-lifes hanging on lighted street lamps and peeking out of alleys.

Cab whizzes along, things start to blur.

Twenty minutes and several miles later. George points to the left.

A CVS sign. Cab pulls over!

Bars on the windows, two armed guards inside.

Pharmacist looks at prescription and says, "You're at the wrong pharmacy. This was called in to the one across town."

Checks address on computer, tells cabbie where it is. Blast off.

Retrace steps, wave at old friends still sinning, arrive at intended CVS. Three blocks from hotel. Who knew?

One prescription, two CVS's, at least twenty miles and fifty minutes later George knocks on hotel room door.

"Gosh, you were gone a long time. I thought it was just around the block?"

"I'm lucky I still have my pants on." Huh? "I'll tell you later."

I popped a pill in my mouth and got into bed.

Ten minutes later I'm sound asleep.

George is wide-awake, reading chapter one of the mindless novel.

9:00 am. I wake up, groggy, get dressed to meet Patsy for breakfast and get to rehearsal.

"Are you OK? You look a little pale," said Patsy, standing at bottom of escalator.

"Oh, I'm fine, just didn't get much sleep." Tell you later.

Make 11:00 am rehearsal in West Garden Court, marble-columned concert space.

Thought this was Washington, not Greece.

No chairs yet. Will be put in before concert.

Temporary stage in place with entrance from hallway that leads to bowels of museum.

Start first few measures of several pieces. Don't want to sing much. Save voice for concert.

Lots of reverb. Nice piano. Patsy happy. I'm happy, still a little groggy.

Afternoon rest in the hotel. Try to nap. No deal.

Arrive at museum early to warm up in green room. Feel pretty good. Excited. Can hear audience buzz from hallway.

Showtime! Enter through slit in curtain to thunderous applause.

People everywhere, in lined-up chairs on several levels to back of vast hall, peering around palms and columns.

Surprise! Nobody said part of the audience would be on stage. Shock. Smile.

Entire stage filled, people on all sides, chairs almost touching the piano.

People close enough to feel my breath, close enough to make Patsy wonder if her bra strap was showing, close enough to be touched when she went for a low note on the piano, so close she couldn't move the bench back as far as she'd like it from the keyboard.

Intermission, relax, it's all good. They loved the Duparc and Boulanger, laughed at the funny Ives pieces and clapped forever after the Vercoe—some wild tempos there, raced to the end.

Learn at intermission that reviewer from Washington Post is sitting behind Patsy's right shoulder, fixed on her hands. Comforting news!

Second half feels even better, energy really high now, ensemble purely in sync, fabulous audience response to Samuel and Bolcom pieces.

Glad crying babies from first half went home to take nap.

We survived and thrived! Still laughing about the day, the three of us drink a toast to Washington, DC, nightlife.

ELEVEN

In Sickness or in Health

The single most difficult issue I had to deal with in my performing life was overcoming several health issues that drained my energy, caused mental and physical stress, and required professional assistance along with a good deal of support from family and friends to continue. As you will read in these diary entries, there were many times when I felt that I might need to throw in the towel and stop trying to move forward with my career on a regular basis. But I will state, without hesitation, that it was the act of singing that brought me back to life and sustained me through the most horrible times. Once I could reconnect with my singing voice, my body and mind seemed to lighten and say, "We can face this. Keep up the good fight." Every singer has to decide when the challenge is too great and the rewards too small to keep singing, but in my case, singing was a lifesaver. A constant positive attitude adjustment, the help of a sturdy and knowledgeable support system, and excellent vocal training were things that I relied on to take me to the levels of performance achievement that I desired when physical adversity crossed my path. If any link in that chain had been weak, I don't know that I would have been able to sing as long as I have.

Recently, I watched a television interview with a spry centenarian who appeared much younger than her age. It was obvious that she looked at life with a quirky sense of humor, since she generated laughter from the audience with her response to every question from the host. When he asked about her secret to living such a long life, she said, "Well, I laugh a lot, I've never been sick, don't take any medications, and never been in the hospital. I guess I have good genes." It would be fantastic if every singer could be like that: have perfect health, enjoy a great sense of humor about life, and never give a thought whether a performance might have to be canceled due to illness. I have known singers who profess to

143

never having had as much as a cold or any other illness that derailed their performing life for even an instant. But that is rare. Most performers are like other humans and have health issues that cause them to need down-time to recuperate.

People react to these short, necessary illness recuperation breaks from daily routine in different ways. It seems to be like aging—some give in to the process and go with the flow, and others fight it every step of the way, determined to delay the inevitable. Personality type, psychological needs, and occupation probably play into a person's reaction to the onset of an illness. I have two friends—they are not performers—one male and one female, who seem to cope extremely well when indisposition rears its ugly head. They appear to delight in what they call their "happy" time, waiting out some malady or recovering from a medical procedure. One fairly beams when describing her days of lounging around, not thinking about anything important for several days, and getting more attention at home than usual. She even speaks of hospital stays as though they were waited-on-hand-and-foot vacations. Unbelievable!

I confess that I am of the opposite type and have no rapport with that kind of thinking. Unless I am truly bedridden and cannot function in any sort of normal manner, I begrudge every moment away from the things I love most—singing, teaching, being among students and friends—and do everything possible to recuperate in as short a span as possible. I also feel an urgency to get back in touch with my voice, to know that it is still there, waiting to emerge again. I suspect that many performers are in my camp. We worry if the voice is affected by some physical problem, and we are not happy until we are certain it is still with us. Also, if performers have upcoming concerts scheduled, they do not have the luxury of enjoying taking time off due to illness, since the longer the voice sits dormant, the longer it takes to get it back in top performing condition.

Singers have to contend with a myriad of health issues. Some of which may directly affect their instrument and its use, such as upper respiratory infections, sinusitis, laryngitis, bronchitis, and strep throat. These kinds of illnesses are usually short-lived and transitory, if caught and treated in time. Still, a singer may need to cease all vocalization to give the voice time to recover before singing full voice and for the length of time required for rehearsals or performances. Performers tend not to be patient patients when it comes to the inability to use the voice. But care must be taken not to force the voice to perform when it is screaming "no." If the voice does not improve significantly within a few days, professional medical advice should be sought to make sure that it is on the path to recovery before pushing it to perform. To do otherwise might cause damage to the vocal cords, require medical intervention and long-term vocal rest, or even mean the end to a career.

Unfortunately, some performers have severe or lingering illnesses that make it difficult to develop and maintain a prolific performing life due to constant debilitation of one kind or another. If an illness becomes chronic, affects the voice negatively, or takes away physical energy, it may become impossible to count on the body and voice to function well on a regular basis. This kind of situation can cause immense anxiety and make a performer have to cut performance dates to a minimum or leave the profession altogether due to uncertainty and constant worry about health issues. It's sad when that has to happen, but for some, it cannot be avoided.

I've taught singers at various levels of training who battled severe asthma, reflux, depression, bipolar disorder, diabetes, hypothyroidism, and other debilitating ailments that made it difficult to maintain a regular rehearsal or travel schedule to keep concert engagements. They were such brave and determined souls, inspiring in their love of the art of singing and their zeal to forge onward in the face of tribulation. Many of them kept going—and were successful—due to an overwhelming love of singing and the discovery of regimens, lifestyle changes, or medications that allowed them to continue, while others found that mistrust and doubt at being in top form brought too much anxiety to continue in the profession. Each singer has to weigh the pros and cons of the performing life with any serious concerns about health, to judge whether concert dates and rehearsals can be kept and whether stamina will be sufficient to perform well under physical and mental duress.

I recall an insightful, intelligent young singer with an extraordinary voice who studied with me during her undergraduate years at the university where I teach. During her first two years there, she was plagued with one illness after another, including asthma. Though she used her voice well, never forced it to perform, and had no discernible technique or vocal cord problems, she was often too ill to sing on master classes or scheduled recitals. She focused on eating well, getting plenty of rest, and taking good care of her body with appropriate exercise but just couldn't seem to achieve a consistent flow of optimum health. It was obvious that frustration was taking a toll and causing her to feel depressed that she could never seem to be in excellent health for every performance date. One day, she came to her lesson and told me that she had decided that, even though singing was her first love, she was going to stop being a voice major and go into another profession. She felt that it would be too difficult and stressful to contend with the uncertainty of her health and its effects on her ability to perform to continue in the singing profession. I understood completely and did not try to dissuade her, having watched her struggle. She still sings beautifully but is now happier as a physician, using her voice only as an avocation, no longer having to deal with the pressure to perform on cue.

There is another side to this issue that must be considered. Do singing and the performing lifestyle have a positive or negative effect on health issues? That is a question that each singer must decide for oneself. The answer depends on the illness—how well it can be managed, how it affects the voice and physical energy, and how much mental stress it causes. It is also important to consider the singer's personality type, which might affect how much stress the singer is able and willing to endure and how that stress can be channeled into something positive for the performing arena.

For many people—whether performers or not—the act of singing brings relief from depression experienced by being sidelined by illness, speeds up the healing process, generates a lasting sense of well-being, and increases mental and physical energy. I am definitely among this group and have experienced all of those positive effects from singing when benched by a physical ailment. This is not a placebo effect. A great deal of research has shown that the act of singing can actually make you feel better. The benefits of singing are extraordinary whether you can carry a tune or not, and they have produced improvement in many kinds of physical ailments. Drs. Mehmet Oz and Michael Roizen, as well as other prominent physicians, recommend it on their health-related websites and in other writings to lower blood pressure, boost a feel-good hormone called oxytocin, improve breathing for those with chronic obstructive pulmonary disease, rewire the brain after a stroke, calm the sympathetic nervous system after a trauma such as cancer treatment, improve cardiac output, relieve stress, and jump-start the immune system. It is also showing great potential to improve cognitive, physical, and emotional benefits for seniors and those with Alzheimer's disease. So, for performers who are plagued by a chronic illness that does not directly affect the vocal cords, singing may be the very best thing for them.

Sometimes an illness can creep up on you. During a two-month period in the spring of 1999, I was engaged to sing with orchestras in Nashville and Virginia and present recitals in New York and Tennessee, including the premiere of a song cycle. No two events contained the same repertoire. Therefore, any spare time that I had available was taken up with rehearsals for the next concert. I was also teaching. So, when I began to feel more tired than usual, I thought it was obvious that I was doing too much with too little time to rest in between. I made it to the end of that series, vowing never again to schedule that many events in such a short span of time. But after a few weeks, I felt more tired than before, quite unlike myself. It is a miracle that I made it through all of those performances intact and in good voice. It turned out that I was experiencing a bout of chronic fatigue caused by hypothyroidism and an attack of the Epstein-Barr virus. My doctor said that it had probably been coming on for some time and—knowing me well—pointed out that it was my usual stubborn personality that wouldn't let me give in to it until the concert dates were over. I don't recommend this approach and should have sought advice sooner.

Due to the onslaught of these three energy-zapping conditions that hit me all at once, it took almost two years to get my physical and mental strength back to a level that I would call normal. It was during that time that I began to work with tai chi, made dietary changes, and followed my physician's advice to add dietary and herbal supplements, which have become such a great benefit for me to regain and maintain energy for daily living. But between 2000 and 2002, I did not sing publicly at all or practice on a regular basis. I simply had no energy to do it, as the brain fog caused by my ailment made it difficult to concentrate and the thyroid disorder changed the quality and stamina of my voice for a time. However, after a few months of silence, I gradually began to realize that to recover from this malady, I needed to find my voice. So, I began to hum softly several times a day, moving into simple vocalises, nothing formal and never at the piano, but just trying to locate that part of me that I missed so much. The act of singing made me feel better physically and forget the low energy accompanied by aches and pains. I listened to some of my old recordings to hear the sound of my voice when it was at its best, recalling how it felt to sing as I once had. It boosted my spirits so much that I began to sing with the recordings, little by little, until one day I knew that my voice was there, strong and sounding much as it had before. This pushed me to reconnect with my accompanist and start rehearsing again on a regular basis to reenter the world of professional singing. Our first performance was local and short but showed me that I was able to continue to do what I loved most. Many professional engagements and two recordings have occurred since that time.

Other than that two-year hiatus, I've been very fortunate in that I've had to cancel a scheduled performance only three times in my career. Two were related to upper respiratory infections, and one was a bout of shingles. Yikes! No fun there. That is rather amazing given the other health issues that I had to surmount at various times during much of my performing career, when physical illness unrelated to my voice made it difficult to go on. In those cases, perhaps I should have canceled. But my "never give up until you are dead" type A personality would not let me do that—for better or for worse. I always instinctively felt that if I could sing, I would feel better overall. It seemed in each case that, though somewhat physically impaired, the act of singing and the exultation I felt at being able to retrieve my voice gave me a much-needed boost to forge onward and overcome the illness that was causing me problems. Without this performance outlet, I believe that my illnesses would not have been tolerated as well.

Though I continued singing through physically challenging times during the last twenty years, I came to realize that I would need to limit the number of engagements that I accepted due to chronic illnesses and full-time teaching. To do otherwise would have drained my energy even further. So, though my performance resume is quite lengthy, I love singing so much that I would have performed even more if able to do so without physical distress. I found the limit that I could bear and still enjoy the performance outlet that I craved. But none of it could have been accomplished without a tremendous amount of support and planning.

CHOOSE PETS CAREFULLY

I have always been a dog lover, thought of them as part of my family, and never really had an altercation with one until 1989 when my lovable peek-a-poo Guido d'Arezzo—named for the medieval music theorist who invented modern music notation—became possessed by a demon and turned into a monster. According to the vet, he had bad genes. One morning about two weeks before I was scheduled to sing a recital at the University of Alabama, I picked Guido up to put him in his little room while I got dressed for the day. Instead of our usual cuddle, I leaned toward him, and suddenly Guido bit-a de mezzo. I dropped him like a rock and knew instinctively that this was going to be bad. Oh my goodness . . .

* * *

Dear Diary,
   March . . . two weeks before recital . . . resting in bed at home
   Got to get well fast.
   Remember shock at looking in mirror.
   Right side of lip completely severed and sliced down an inch or more toward chin.
   "George, call the doctor. Guido bit me."
   Blood everywhere. Press towel tightly over wound.
   Doctor on phone, listening to description. "Doesn't sound too bad," he says.
   Get to hospital now, he'll meet us there.
   Waiting room, fifteen minutes, in comes doctor.
   Takes one look at gaping wound and says, "I can't fix this. Only one person in Clarksville who can."
   If not in his office, it's off to plastic surgeon in Nashville. Groan.
   I wait. Good news. New doctor strides into emergency room.
   Looks me over, smiles and says, "Well, this is going to be interesting. I haven't done this kind of work since Vietnam."
   Lying on table, face numb from local anesthetic, tetanus shot, and reassurance.
   Two doctors peering down, talking about other cases, one delicately working magic in three-layer stitches.
   An hour-and-a-half go by. Waiting for verdict, trying not to move.

"Almost done. It's looking good," he says.

"When will I be able to sing? I've got a concert to do in two weeks."

"You shouldn't be thinking about that now." Gives instructions.

"Don't move mouth or open too wide. Will pull apart stitches and won't heal well.

Come see me in a week to take out the stitches. We'll go from there."

High-powered antibiotics knock me out.

* * *

Two weeks later . . . after concert . . . Birmingham

Fantastic audience, full house.

Lovely reception after concert.

Face still a little puffy.

"What happened?" asked one student, pointing to my chin.

I explain. She looks faint!

Happy with concert. No glitches. Amazing.

Only rehearsed music once in last two weeks, yesterday.

Glad resident composer, Fred Goossen, liked interpretation of his songs.

Thought I'd never be able to do this.

Took awhile to recover from trauma and onslaught of heavy dose of antibiotics.

No singing or opening mouth wide for ten days.

Stitches removed. Replaced by tiny adhesive tapes, almost unnoticeable.

Genius doctor. Says it should heal without a scar. Sure am glad he made it out of Vietnam.

* * *

KNOW YOUR BLOOD TYPE

Somewhere around age thirty-eight, my body seemed to flip a switch and decide to malfunction—perhaps those bad genes kicked in—and I was plagued by years of severe anemia caused by uncontrollable heavy menstrual periods. This kind of personal, sometimes embarrassing and difficult-to-manage condition is one that many singers deal with regularly but rarely gets discussed, except in medical journals or the doctor's office. Often, there is a lack of understanding and support from those most directly involved with a singer's performing life. Thus, singers often suffer in silence, reluctant to talk about it. No one likes to divulge these kinds of matters unless absolutely necessary. I have spoken with female singers who were shocked at the response when they had to cancel a rehearsal or performance due to incapacitation caused by this problem and were expected to tell a voice teacher, coach, or manager the reason. In one case, a soprano was told that if something as frivolous as this was going to bother her, she was just too fragile for a performance career and should either get over it or get out of the profession. Another singer's concerns were dismissed altogether, told that it was all in her head and what she really needed was a psychiatrist. These insensitive, uninformed remarks and attitudes should not be accepted nor tolerated when faced with debilitating conditions that prevent one from enjoying a harmonious creative life. Instead, strategies should be discussed concerning ways to surmount this predicament.

It is hard to get on with life as usual, when daily routine is arduous, making every decision or activity a chore. Over a period of eight years and with the consultation of nine different doctors, no cause or solution was found for me, though many treatments were tried. Eventually, it was decided that a hysterectomy was the only answer, since I was finding it more and more difficult to cope with the physical weakness and life-threatening severity of my condition. Much of my performing career took place during that time, though it was often a struggle, since anemia causes fatigue, heart palpitations, difficulty in concentrating and headaches, among other symptoms, all of which I experienced from time to time. Living on iron pills for years, I would go up and down in energy and have times when my red blood cells were so hard to find that my doctor once considered putting me in the hospital for a transfusion. So, this kind of sickness is no joke and not just in someone's head when it happens. It affects everything she does and certainly drains her energy to be in top form.

When faced with an ordeal such as this, each singer must decide for herself the amount of travel, rehearsal time, and stress she is able to endure to fulfill her performance schedule. It is important that the decision be an informed one, in consultation with doctors and her support system, to be sensible about the continuation of a busy performance routine. But no one should be bullied either to continue or not to continue due to the lack of understanding and flexibility of those with whom the singer works or studies.

During my eight-year period of malaise, I continued to perform at regional, national, and international venues and made three recordings. However, when I look back on a few of those events, I wonder how in the world I was able to dredge up the energy and fortitude to get through them. I drew heavily on my acting skills and positive-thinking mantras and never let the audience in on my secret distress. I believe that in each case, the musical, vocal, and emotional outcomes were positive and that once I finally got on the stage and started singing, I could feel the physical and mental energy build throughout the performance so that by the time I got to the end, I felt much better than I had when I began. It's amazing what the act of singing can do for the spirit and the sense of well-being.

Part of the maddening uncertainty of my ailment was the fact that it would miraculously get better for a few months—making me think it had resolved—only to reappear in a spectacular way just when I was about to sing a major concert. I remember one regional National Association of Teachers of Singing guest recital when . . .

* * *

Dear Diary,

   Richmond . . . hotel room . . . night before concert

Got to Nashville airport early. Felt a little weak. Sat down to wait for Patsy.

Had a bad night. Monthly demon returned full force two days ago.

"You look pale," said Patsy.

"I'll be ok. Just have to get some energy back."

Boarded plane. Drank plenty of water. Closed eyes to rest and relax.

Felt dizzy. Put head down on lap. "Can I help?" Patsy worried.

Surroundings felt unreal, going to pass out.

Got stewardess's attention. Helped me to back of plane.

Lay down in empty seats on last row 'til plane landed.

Drank more water. Cold cloths. Two stewardesses hovering. So nice!

Somehow got to hotel, don't remember taxi.

Face ashen. Have to go to bed. Everything a blur.

Too weak to make 4:00 rehearsal in concert hall.

Stayed in bed while Patsy checked out piano and acoustics.

Will have to sing cold. Can't think about that now.

Dinner sent up from hotel restaurant. Nibbled a little, no appetite.

Have to rest. Not able to move. Hard to breathe.

* * *

Next day . . . after concert . . . hotel room . . . getting ready for bed.

Stayed in bed all day until time to get dressed.

Ate two small meals in room. Felt a little stronger.

Patsy trying not to look worried, afraid I'd faint again.

Can't believe concert went so well.

Most surreal performance of career. On autopilot.

No memory lapses and voice felt strong.

Was it real or imagined? Maybe a dream, if so, a good dream.

Enthusiastic audience of students and voice teachers.

Back at hotel fell onto bed in relief and joy of survival.

Hunger!!! Now I can eat. Order and devour giant hamburger and fries.

11:00 pm. Phone call from hotel lounge.

Small group of voice teachers invite us to come down for drinks and celebrate concert.

Enjoyed camaraderie, but exhausted.

Complimented me on unusual, difficult program. Doubt they knew the half of it.

* * *

DON'T PANIC

Sometimes, a debilitating physical condition is forced on you by accident or circumstance, and as hard as you try, it affects every aspect of your existence, including your performing life. That is what happened to me in the spring of 1991 when life as I knew it changed. As I have already mentioned, I had been experiencing major bouts of anemia due to blood loss but always managed to keep going with the support of personal physicians.

One weekend in March of that year, I became so weak that I ended up in the emergency room of the local hospital. As fate would have it, both of my doctors were out of town on vacation. I was seen by a physician who did not know my medical history or me or the fact that my body tends not to like medications. He recommended a medical procedure that required sedation, but as soon as lactated Ringer's (a commonly used solution) was put into the IV, my entire body started to shut down. Unfortunately, those in charge did not assume that the solution was causing my problem, so they continued to give me the drug by IV for almost four hours. This caused total paralysis (I could move only my lips). However, I was fully awake during all of the commotion, consternation, and discussion about what might be causing this and what to do. It was incredibly frightening. I could feel great panic inside my body but couldn't move. After episodes of crash carts and hovering doctors, they finally stopped giving me the drug, since no medical procedures could be done and I began to revive slightly, enough to go home . . . so they said. Thus, I was dismissed from the hospital with final words from the nurse, who rolled my wheelchair to the car, saying, "You really need to learn to calm down so that things like this don't happen." Obviously, I paralyzed myself for six hours—not a good thought to leave in a patient's mind after such a disaster.

I survived that episode, barely, and saw my regular physician a week later in his office to discuss what had happened to me. He was most sympathetic and said that only one in a million are allergic or especially sensitive to this particular substance, but I happened to be that one. He also said it was a miracle my body survived the onslaught of the drug for that many hours. That compliment did not make me feel any better about the episode. I was still very weak and feeling extremely nervous almost all of the time. I couldn't sleep without waking startled.

Over the next few weeks, I gained physical strength, but the trauma of the emergency and its possible consequence caused me to develop severe panic attacks and have flashbacks of the ordeal. Eventually, I feared getting outside my house or driving my car by myself. This was not like me. It was unthinkable that I might become agoraphobic, unable to teach or sing in public again. I could not let this happen. I have always been a people person, not a stay-at-home and hide-away type. So, when this event occurred that made me shun going outside my house, I had to gather up every bit of courage I could find to get back to what I considered normal, to enjoy daily life and continue to have a concert career.

I was scheduled to sing a recital and do several days of master classes at the University of Arkansas, Little Rock, early that summer. I was determined not to cancel. So, I had only a few weeks to recuperate, get my voice back (I had not been singing at all, too consumed with the effects of the trauma), and travel there. Just the thought of going there by myself gave me a panic attack. But, I decided to . . .

* * *

Dear Diary,
   May . . . six weeks before Arkansas trip
   Feel doomed, depressed, stuck.
   Need to go and sing. Got to get back to normal.
   Several hours drive there. Can I do it alone?
   Panic, hands shaking.
   "Walk around, get rid of adrenaline overload," doctor said.
   Must go and sing! Got to get out of house.
   Where's my support system?
   George has other obligations, can't go and stay four days.
   Patsy will meet me there day before recital. Can't go with me.
   I'll drive by myself. Panic!!! Can't do it.
   Can't give in to this. Divert attention. Go shopping.
   Can't even do that. Panic in car on way to mall, turn around, come home.
   Doctor suggests medication for anxiety. I resist. Hate pills.
   Already tried acupuncture, talk, talk, talk, and meditation. None help.
   Exercise made it worse.
   Singing again, voice still there. Feels good to express in tones again.
   Performance thoughts. Panic bubbling up inside.
   A panic attack in the middle of the concert! What if?
   Will call former student, now friend, about going with me.
   Can't go alone. I'll never make it without panic.
   Have to solve this!

* * *

Little Rock . . . hotel room . . . after concert

Arrived just fine with generous friend from Nashville.

Agreed to drive my car here and back to Clarksville.

Friend spent two days at pool and mall while I taught master classes.

Left yesterday when Patsy arrived for rehearsal.

"That's the best you've sung in years. I can't believe you could do it," said Patsy.

Relief! Concert went beautifully. Appreciative audience.

Lovely reception with faculty. Lots of laughter.

Felt good out there on the stage. No panic. Body and mind in high gear.

Doctor adamant. "Now Sharon, some people have to take pills for high blood pressure and others have to take pills for anxiety. So, get over it."

And I did. Glad I gave in to doctor's insistence. Still, not without a fight.

A lifesaver. Couldn't have come without them.

What a support system! I felt secure, panic never surfaced.

Now, I won't be a flight risk.

TWELVE

Surprise!

Sometimes, it's the little things that make a performing life so much fun and so memorable: the offbeat things people say, the dress hems that get caught on nails as you approach the stage, the insects that fly into your mouth—after circling your head for three minutes—when taking a deep breath to sing with an orchestra during an outdoor concert, the sudden realization that one earring has dropped off somewhere between the dressing room and the stage entrance, having to leave your room for hours when the hotel kitchen catches on fire, the worry about your pregnant accompanist who is eating crackers right up until she walks onto the stage so as not to throw up on the piano, or the lawnmowers that roar past open windows of the concert hall during your afternoon recital.

All of those strange things and more have occurred in my performing life. I'm sure that every singer who has been performing for a good while could fill a book with peculiar remembrances that bring on a laugh or a groan. It's all part of this wonderful, haphazard life of the performing artist. I wouldn't take anything for having experienced them. Each one had a quirky element that contributed to the event itself and has given those of us involved much cause for laughter over the years.

There are many other favorite memories of concerts that contained surprises of one kind or another, like the time I programmed Samuel Barber's song "A Green Lowland of Pianos," which ends with a double repetition of the words "black pianos." In this case, the normal black concert grand had been replaced with a surprisingly unusual white grand, the only one I've ever performed with. It made the song even more humorous than intended and was much appreciated by the audience.

Then, there was the concert at the beautiful Cheekwood Botanical Gardens and Museum of Art in Nashville. I had no idea until I arrived for the performance that sections of the museum had been renovated a few days prior to the event. As we entered the concert space, sawdust glinted in the sunlight coming through the windows, and every breath provided a challenge not to sneeze or cough. I made it all the way through the new song cycle I was singing until the last piece, when the pent-up sneezes would wait no longer. Some things just can't be avoided, so sneeze I did, not once but four times in shotgun fashion. The audience let out with sympathetic applause, nods of the head, and a few delicate giggles, since most of them had been sneezing already.

Oh, yes, there was that time when my briefcase disappeared at an international music festival. I had left it backstage on a table while rehearsing in the concert hall and found it missing when I went to retrieve it. I was frantic because it contained all of my music, some of which I needed for this performance, plus my only copy of the score to an upcoming premiere. I hated the thought of having to call the composer to say that I had lost his precious music—not a good impression to make. I searched everywhere, asked everyone, including all the performers, but no one seemed to have seen it. I made copies from my accompanist's scores of the three pieces I needed for this performance. But since the new piece was for orchestra and did not involve her, she had no rehearsal copy. So, I contemplated the dreaded phone call to the composer. Happily, there was a turn of events. Two days later, one of the other singers brought the briefcase to me with an apology, saying it looked just like hers—therefore, she didn't realize that she had mine until she opened it to get out her own music the night before. I was relieved to find it. From that day on, I never let my music or briefcase out of my sight at any concert venue.

FRIEND A PIANO TECHNICIAN

I get to carry my instrument around with me for better or for worse. But my accompanists have always had to deal with whatever piano was available at the various venues at which we performed. Most were gems, but some needed to be read the last rites. And in one case, my accompanist decided that the venue itself had bad karma for her. We performed there twice, about eight years apart, using two different pianos, and chaos was the result each time. The first time . . .

* * *

Dear Diary,
    A university in the South . . . late '80s
    First time we've had a piano unravel during a concert.
    Should sign it up for Social Security.

Soft, rat-like scratching sound started on the second Ives piece.
He would have loved it. Eccentric fellow.
First break in program. Backstage. Musing about strange sound.
"I think there's something alive in that piano."
"Maybe a part is about to fall off, you think?"
Back out on stage.
More excitement. Audience seems to love it.
Loud squeak, followed by bing, bing, bing in middle of Rochberg piece.
It's contemporary music, but those sounds are a little too weird.
Wouldn't love this. He's not that eccentric.
Intermission.
"That was a unique sound. Never heard anything like that."
"It's the sostenuto pedal. Something's wrong with it."
"Can you play the rest without using it?"
"Not sure. You seem to find a lot of music that requires it."
Second half going spiffily.
Ow! Extremely loud clank in middle of Mary Howe piece.
Great acoustics. Heads perk up on back row. Necks crane forward.
Offstage.
Short break before final songs. Trying to hold in laughter.
"What was that? Nice diversion just before the high note."
"The sostenuto pedal fell off. I shoved it under the piano with my left foot. Glad I don't need it for the Vercoe."

* * *

Same university . . . eight years later . . . after concert
"I guess I'm hard on pianos," Patsy says, getting into car.
Gales of laughter. Gasp, can't talk.
Can't believe it happened again.
Same school, different piano.
New Steinway this time, bravo for them.
Walked out for first piece, full house. Thunderous applause.
Piano bench too low. Wait a minute.
Patsy rolls knobs forward. Good to go.
Duparc and Fauré beautiful, lots of flow, simpatico ensemble.
Audience really into the Vehar pieces.
Intermission.
Backstage. Happy, so far.
"That bench is still too low. I'll adjust it a little more when we go back out."
"Sure, that's fine. Take your time."
Walk, applause, smile, bow, wait.
Patsy rolls knobs slightly forward.

Clank!!! Knob on right side of bench rolls off onto floor and under piano.

Slight gasp from audience left.

Great lead-in for Bolcom's "Over the Piano." He would love this. Quirky composer.

Don't dare look around. Smile. Just keep singing.

* * *

RECORD AT YOUR OWN RISK

I've always had a certain reverence for professional recordings—those magical moments in time when a performer's flawless technique is captured exquisitely, to be remembered for posterity as a perfect replica of one's inexplicable, sophisticated sense of divine interpretation spontaneously produced at every performance. Sure. That's what I used to think until I made eight recordings. The excitement and anticipation of one's first recording are palpable. All you think about is the fact that your voice is finally going to be out there for the world to hear how wonderful you really are. Immortality is an addictive thing. Never mind the windup to the final product—and there is quite a windup involved.

In 1983, when I recorded my first LP (*long-playing* record, for those under forty), I knew that it would be recorded in a concert hall that I had performed in, that it was scheduled to be completed over a period of two days, and that the person who would be recording it was my husband, who has some of the best musical ears in the business and knows my voice better than anyone. But I was not mentally prepared for the exhausting process of setting mics in just the right place to get the best sound, moving the piano to at least five different places on the stage before settling on the right one, or performing the number of takes necessary due to outside noises and a loud air-conditioning system that had to be dealt with before continuing to record. All I wanted to do was sing, not stand around. It was a tiring, confusing process.

By the end, I really didn't know how I sounded. I would stop and listen to myself on headphones after each take and be asked, "Is that good enough to go on to the next song?" That's a very hard decision to make, since each one sounded very much like the last, except there was this note or two that might be just a little off center or a little late off the beat, something trivial, but how to decide which one is best? All spontaneity had disappeared from the performance. Now everything became a plan of attack to fix that particular note or give a little more time to one individual rest. Everything seemed to be mechanical. The inspiration that I started with had disappeared and was hard to dredge up by the end of the two-day session. I was starting to doubt the whole process. Had we made a good recording or not? I really didn't know.

I was further dismayed on a subsequent visit with a consulting recording engineer in Nashville who asked during the editing process, "How do you want to sound?" In my naïve world, I assumed that I would sound like myself, of course. "But," he says, "I can tweak this a little here and turn that mic down a little there, maybe bring up the room ambience a little more in that spot or color your voice brighter or darker, and give it more space or less space." He showed me at least ten ways to change the quality of my voice. None of them sounded like the way I think I really sound. The more he fiddled with the sound, the less I could recognize myself. I listened intently and kept saying that I just wanted to hear my own voice, no tweaking. I stood my ground, and in the end, we used the original tracks that had been laid down, no tweaking. All he did was edit the tape to send to the record company. The result was pretty much what I wanted, and that recording got rave reviews for sound engineering.

That first recording took place when things were recorded on tape. Today, with digital technology, there are many more possibilities for reinventing the sound of a person's voice and performance ability. Does anyone really sound like oneself anymore? I wonder. I've had students who go to concerts to hear a famous singer whose recordings they have devoured, only to be disappointed when the voice wasn't quite what they heard on the CD or, heaven forbid, the performer made a few musical or memory errors. After all, the CD they had listened to ad nauseam was a perfect replica of that performer's ability 100 percent of the time, right? There is no telling how many repetitions and edits it took to get it right on that CD. Individual notes can be made to sound on pitch when they were not; rhythms can be adjusted to fit when they didn't; time between notes can be taken out if needed; and a multitude of other kinds of edits can be made to perfect the performance.

My subsequent experiences with recording were similar to the first one in that it was difficult to make decisions about track choices for the final cuts. After a while, either they all start to sound alike as you get more and more confused about which one to choose, or depression sets in that none of them truly reflects what you thought you had done in the recording session. In one case, the overall quality of the recording I made was not at all what I expected because the mic had been placed too close to my mouth and there was not enough room ambiance in the overall sound, making the voice appear brittle in quality—something that was not discovered until after the session was completed, with no opportunity nor funds for a redo. This problem had been difficult to detect when listening to takes over the headphones. When I made a different recording some years later, the piano ended up sounding like it was in a cave because the engineer decided to cover the bombastic Bösendorfer with a rug, since he couldn't figure out how to get the balance he wanted through mic placement. Ugh! That was very disappointing for the pianist and made the voice sound as if it were being recorded in a separate room from the piano—not what we were trying to achieve.

There is also something psychological that happens when a microphone is placed in front of you and the engineer motions for silence in preparation for the recording to begin. Suddenly, the word *perfect* begins to pass in front of your eyes and ramble through your brain as if on ticker tape. It is never ending, just scrolling right along the bottom of your invisible screen while you sing. There is a sense that every breath, sound, color, and nuance in your voice is caught in a small box that can't be opened too wide or it might let out something obscene that will be recorded for university vocal majors and critics of the future to rail against. Once the thought of perfection becomes lodged in your mind, the word *spontaneous* has no application to the process, and everything that happens from that point on seems forced.

It took some time for me to reconcile all of this psychological baggage that I was putting on myself. But by the time I was engaged in my third recording, I realized that it was best to think of the first take of each piece as if it were the final and only take. I would visualize performing in a concert setting with an audience and not consider that I would need to do it again. That seemed to help quite a bit. I was able to be in the moment longer and center on the musical performance rather than judge what someone might think of the performance thirty years from now. However, that desire for perfection never really goes away, and it wreaks havoc when least expected. I was in the middle of recording Elizabeth Vercoe's fabulous monodrama *Herstory III: Jehanne de Lorraine* with Rosemary Platt for the Owl label when . . .

* * *

Dear Diary,
After recording session . . . all takes finished . . . exhausted.
Love, love, love this piece!
Has it all; drama, pathos, intimacy, spoken dialog, exotic vocal and piano effects.
Long and demanding. Thirty-minute work. No place to rest. Hard to record.
Concentrate. Keep voice fluid. Use speaking voice in proper register.
Voice tired now. No more singing today or tomorrow.
Watch Rosemary gather up gear. Needs an assistant!
Lots of paraphernalia—gong, mallets, finger cymbals, triangle beaters, wood blocks.
Not just playing piano keys on this one.
Requires organization and intricate placement of equipment.
Sitting on edge of piano bench, leaned against wall. I can't move.
Legs tired from standing all day.

Not one ounce of energy left.

Engineer packing up. "Goodbye."

He'll send us the takes to choose from.

Oh, and the composer will get a listen, too.

Sounds good. Can't wait to hear it.

Got everything done. Worn out mentally and physically.

Five hours of tension, too long. Seemed longer.

Can't believe it took fourteen takes to get "God Be in My Head" right.

That high A flat usually just floats out. Actually did float out on the first take.

Had to redo. Mallet fell off piano onto floor in next to last bar.

"Cut."

Aargh!!!!

Takes two through five aborted due to clock tower striking ten, a vocal tone that I hated, some vibration of the concert hall window, and a mis-sung word on the third page.

"Cut, cut, cut." Oh, and "cut."

I now despise all A flats and declare, "The longer you sing this piece, the tighter you get."

Not sure what happened after that until take twelve when perfection occurred.

Glee. We both knew it.

Rosemary prepared to play her last note, leaned to the right on the piano bench and it gave out a long, agonizing squeak.

"Cut."

[*Expletives deleted.*]

Take thirteen never made it out of the gate.

At that point, a miracle happened. We did it. Take fourteen, a winner.

Breath holding until engineer gives signal.

"I wonder if Elizabeth knows how hard this piece is to put together."

Exhale.

* * *

Several weeks later . . . at home . . . listening to takes with Rosemary

Engineer sent copy to make choices from possible takes.

Engineer says he can fix a few things if we want. Take out a little space here, put a little more space there, bring up more room ambience in a few places. Whee!

Just let him know. Won't be a problem.

Says he sent copy to composer for opinion, also.

Excited, but dread first listen. Here we go.

Sit back far enough to take in surround sound.

"This is making me nervous. Don't recognize any of these takes."

"I don't remember that tone sounding so dark."

"Why did I phrase that line that way?"

"This can't be the take we thought was the best. I hate the sound of that high G."

"Surely we didn't put that much rubato in that line?"

"I really like the sound of the finger cymbals. Wish they had a bigger part."

"That gong took on a life of its own."

"I think I like the first take of number five best."

"I thought you hated that one."

"Was that the one I hated?"

Can't decide which take. This is crazy.

Five choices on section number six alone. Each has a problem.

One needs more emotion, two has a note that sounds tentative, three is OK but missing something, four sounds square, and five is too perfect.

Too perfect! We've lost our minds.

Phone rings. Composer calling. Knows we're listening to takes.

"Hi Sharon, I understand that the longer you sing 'God Be in My Head,' the tighter you get." We stare at each other.

He didn't. Yes, he did. He sent her a copy that has everything on it, including what we said between takes.

Glad she has sense of humor.

I just love, love, love this piece!

Appendix: Fifty Practical Pointers for Performers

1. Warm up your voice every day to keep it in shape, especially as you age.
2. Monitor your voice for tiredness, stress, or physical tension.
3. Learn to be patient when developing vocal technique.
4. Become a first-rate musician, not just a singer.
5. Get to know your maintenance level and what you need to succeed.
6. Be passionate about your art.
7. Don't be a diva, but stand up for yourself when necessary.
8. Discover what you perform best, and stick to it.
9. Focus on what you do well, not your faults.
10. Work on your memory for lyrics and the names of people you meet.
11. Believe in luck, and look for it to come your way.
12. Write down the things for which you are grateful each day.
13. Find the best voice teacher or coach possible.
14. Choose compatible musical collaborators.
15. Beware of information overload.
16. Take short brain breaks when you feel stressed or overworked.
17. Choose to think positive thoughts every day.
18. Learn to connect to others through kindness.
19. Work on your speaking voice so that it projects well.
20. Get organized, and visualize what needs to be done to get ahead.
21. Overlearn everything that you are scheduled to perform.
22. Always be on time for auditions, interviews, and rehearsals.
23. Dress for success in interviews, auditions, and performances.
24. Be careful what you say in public places or on social networking.
25. Work on coping skills with talk therapy, meditation, or some other aid.
26. Seek out reputable doctors for general health and voice concerns.
27. Don't allow someone to abuse you or your voice.
28. Make good interpersonal relationships a priority.
29. Cultivate a good support system of friends and advisors.
30. Be compassionate with colleagues.
31. Become an independent thinker, not a clone of someone else.

32. Get inspired by the great performers in your field.
33. Keep your body in good physical shape.
34. Develop a comfortable routine for performance days.
35. Work to be flexible when plans have to change.
36. Get plenty of rest when traveling to perform.
37. Stay hydrated with water when flying on airplanes or rehearsing.
38. Stay away from smoke, dust, and foods that interfere with singing.
39. Monitor your thinking and stay positive with appropriate self-talk.
40. Get away from negative people and situations.
41. Get rid of bad health habits.
42. Develop your sense of humor, and use it as much as possible.
43. Make at least one new career contact every month.
44. Stay in touch with other musicians you meet on the road.
45. Create a workable lifestyle.
46. Learn to relax with enjoyable pastimes.
47. Get outside and enjoy nature.
48. Write down the things that make you happy.
49. Realize that building a career takes perseverance.
50. Learn to laugh and laugh a lot.

Suggested Reading

The following resources are just a starting point for the acquisition of information that will help you become a better, more confident performer. I encourage you to read everything that remotely applies to the performer's life to be better prepared for all that lies ahead. Singers need to be armed with knowledge about their art and have good sources of information concerning the understanding of healthy vocal technique, the elimination of stress, and the development of life strategies that are workable and have the possibility of making every day an extraordinary experience.

I have listed books of several types for various purposes. Some of them focus on the development of vocal technique that includes placement and clarity of tone, vocal freedom, proper breath support, diction, evenness of registration, and other elements that affect the longevity and stamina of a singer's voice. Some provide information about auditions, publicity, management, and other components that are related to the business of performing and how to get ahead of the competition. Still, others give ideas about how to relieve physical and mental tension, live a healthy lifestyle, create a balanced emotional life, or rid the performer of stage fright and anxiety. A few center on the philosophy of performance and artistic endeavors in general, and others are memoirs that relate the performance life from a personal point of view. Each has its place in the performer's library.

Never stop learning, never stop reading, and never stop asking questions. You will be a better performer and a more interesting and intellectually energetic person if you remain a constant learner throughout life, seeking to find something new and exciting every day that you did not know the day before. May your reading bring enlightenment and bliss!

Balk, H. Wesley. *Performing Power: A New Approach for the Singer-Actor.* Minneapolis: University of Minnesota Press, 1986.
Bassett, Lucinda. *Life without Limits.* New York: Cliff Street Books, 2001.
Bayles, David, and Ted Orland. *Art and Fear: Observations on the Perils (and Rewards) of Artmaking.* Santa Barbara, CA: Capra Press, 1997.
Beeching, Angela Myles. *Beyond Talent: Creating a Successful Career in Music.* New York: Oxford University Press, 2010.
Bloodworth, Venice. *Key to Yourself.* Radford, VA: Wilder, 2009.
Cameron, Julia. *The Artist's Way: A Spiritual Path to Higher Creativity.* New York: Tarcher/Putnam, 1992.

Covey, Stephen R. *The Seven Habits of Highly Effective People.* New York: Simon & Schuster, 1989.

Craig, David. *A Performer Prepares.* New York: Applause, 1993.

Cutler, David. *The Savvy Musician: Building a Career, Earning a Living, and Making a Difference.* Pittsburgh, PA: Helius Press, 2010.

Davis, Martha, Elizabeth Robbins Eshelman, and Matthew McKay. *The Relaxation and Stress Reduction Workbook.* Oakland, CA: New Harbinger, 2008.

Dayme, Maribeth Bunch. *The Performer's Voice: Realizing Your Vocal Potential.* New York: Norton, 2006.

Dornemann, Joan. *Complete Preparation: A Guide to Auditioning for Opera.* New York: Excalibur, 1992.

Emmons, Shirlee, and Alma Thomas. *Power Performance for Singers: Transcending the Barriers.* New York: Oxford University Press, 1998.

Fanning, Patrick. *Visualization for Change.* Oakland, CA: New Harbinger, 1994.

Fleming, Renée. *The Inner Voice: The Making of a Singer.* New York: Penguin Books, 2004.

Goleman, Daniel. *Emotional Intelligence.* New York: Bantam Doubleday Dell, 1995.

———. *Working with Emotional Intelligence.* New York: Bantam Books, 1998.

Green, Barry, and Timothy Galwey. *The Inner Game of Music.* New York: Doubleday, 1986.

Hallowell, Edward M. *Crazy Busy: Overstretched, Overbooked, and about to Snap!* New York: Ballantine Books, 2006.

Heirich, Ruby Jane. *Voice and the Alexander Technique: Active Explorations for Speaking and Singing.* Berkeley, CA: Mornum Time Press, 2005.

Highstein, Ellen. *Making Music in Looking Glass Land: A Guide to Survival and Business Skills for the Classical Musician.* New York: Concert Artists Guild, 1993.

Hines, Jerome. *Great Singers on Great Singing.* New York: Limelight Editions, 1982.

Kabat-Zinn, Jon. *Full Catastrophe Living: Using the Wisdom of Your Body and Mind to Face Stress, Pain, and Illness.* New York: Delacorte Press, 1990.

Klickstein, Gerald. *The Musician's Way: A Guide to Practice, Performance, and Wellness.* New York: Oxford University Press, 2009.

Malde, Melissa, Mary Jean Allen, and Kurt-Alexander Zeller. *What Every Singer Needs to Know about the Body.* San Diego, CA: Plural, 2008.

McKinney, James C. *The Diagnosis and Correction of Vocal Faults.* Nashville, TN: Genevox Music Group, 1994.

Miller, Richard. *On the Art of Singing.* New York: Oxford University Press, 2011.

———. *Solutions for Singers: Tools for Performers and Teachers.* New York: Oxford University Press, 2004.

Monahan, Brent. *The Singer's Companion: A Guide to Improving Your Voice and Performance.* Pompton Plains, NJ: Limelight Editions, 2006.

Papolos, Janice. *The Performing Artist's Handbook.* Cincinnati, OH: Writer's Digest Books, 1984.

Pelletier, Kenneth R. *Sound Mind, Sound Body: A New Model for Lifelong Health.* New York: Simon & Schuster, 1994.

Ristad, Eloise. *A Soprano on Her Head: Right-Side-Up Reflections on Life and Other Performances.* Moab, UT: Real People Press, 1982.

Roizen, Michael F., and Mehmet Oz. *You: Stress Less.* New York: Simon & Schuster, 2011.

Tolle, Eckhart. *The Power of Now.* Vancouver, BC: Namaste, 2004.

Ware, Clifton. *Basics of Vocal Pedagogy: The Foundations and Process of Singing.* New York: McGraw-Hill, 1998.

———. *The Singer's Life: Goals and Roles.* Roseville, MN: Birch Grove, 2005.

Weil, Andrew. *Spontaneous Happiness.* New York: Little, Brown, 2011.

Wormhoudt, Pearl S. *With a Song in My Psyche: On the Psychology of Singing and Teaching Singing.* Philadelphia: Xlibris, 2002.

About the Author

Sharon Mabry, mezzo-soprano, first received national recognition in the 1980 National Public Radio *Art of Song* series when she was a featured recitalist. Since then her sensitive interpretation of traditional and contemporary music has placed her in demand as a recitalist, soloist with symphony orchestras, and master teacher of vocal techniques. Mabry has been a frequent guest artist at new music festivals and has presented recitals in major venues, such as Merkin Concert Hall (New York City), the Corcoran Gallery of Art (Washington, DC), the National Gallery of Art (Washington, DC), three national conventions of the National Association of Teachers of Singing, and several of its regional conventions and summer workshops. She has been invited to sing recitals and present master classes at more than forty colleges and universities in the United States and Great Britain and was the recipient of two major grants from the National Endowment for the Arts: a solo recitalist fellowship and a recording grant.

Mabry has premiered works by more than thirty composers and made eight critically acclaimed recordings. Each recording showcased works by contemporary composers or music by women composers. Her latest CDs are *Music by Vercoe, Goossen and Barber*; *Music by Women: A Celebration*; and *Lincoln Portraits*, on which she is the featured soloist with members of the Nashville Symphony Orchestra in Roy Harris's "Abraham Lincoln Walks at Midnight."

In addition to her concert career, Mabry is professor of music at Austin Peay State University, Clarksville, Tennessee, where she received the university's highest award for creativity (the Richard M. Hawkins Award) and that for teaching (the Distinguished Professor Award). From 1985 through 2009, she was a featured writer for the National Association of Teachers of Singing's *Journal of Singing*, the preeminent journal for singers and voice teachers, with her column "New Directions," which discussed trends in contemporary music. Her book *Exploring Twentieth-Century Vocal Music* was published in 2002. She holds a bachelor of music from Florida State University, a master of music and a doctor of musical arts from George Peabody College/Vanderbilt University, and a performance certificate from the prestigious Franz-Schubert-Institut in Austria.